THE *B*

STAND-UP
COMEDY

Bruce Dessau

Bluffer's®

Hammersley House
5-8 Warwick Street
London W1B 5LX
United Kingdom

Email: info@bluffers.com
Website: bluffers.com
Twitter: @BluffersGuide

Published 2014
Copyright © Bluffer's® 2014

Publisher: Thomas Drewry
Publishing Director: Brooke McDonald

Series Editor: David Allsop
Design and Illustration: Jim Shannon

A CIP Catalogue record for this book
is available from the British Library.

Bluffer's Guide®, Bluffer's® and Bluff Your Way®
are registered trademarks.

ISBN: 978-1-909937-24-6 (print)
      978-1-909937-25-3 (ePub)
      978-1-909937-26-0 (Kindle)

CONTENTS

In 2008 researchers concluded that the oldest joke they had found dated from 2000 BC and was a proverb told by the smutty Sumerians of southern Mesopotamia.

A CAVEMAN WALKS
INTO A CAVE...

A veritable plethora of archaeologists and archivists have argued for years about the origins of stand-up comedy. Where did it start? What purpose did it serve? Why did it catch on? Some speculate that the ancient Greeks were the first people to stand on a stage and tell jokes. Others have suggested that, between conquering Europe and Asia Minor, the Romans entertained each other with pithy anecdotes about dissolute emperors making their horses consuls, why their roads had no corner shops, and how the queen of Egypt was such an enthusiastic fellatrix that she once pleasured 100 Roman soldiers in a single session.*

Humour probably goes back to the dawn of civilisation. No sooner had one Neanderthal brought home a dead animal than he was standing around the fire saying something to the effect of 'Don't you just hate it when you go out to hunt a red deer and you get halfway into the forest and can't remember what you went there for?' The others laughed so much that he returned the following week to tell the same story. A month later he had an agent negotiating a tour of nearby caves.

*See *The Bluffer's Guide to Sex* for confirmation.

In 2008 researchers at the University of Wolverhampton (that's not an oxymoron) concluded that the oldest joke they had found dated from 2000 BC and was a proverb told by the smutty Sumerians of southern Mesopotamia: 'Something which has never occurred since time immemorial; a young woman did not fart in her husband's lap.'

The oldest-known recorded English joke dates from Anglo-Saxon times and was found in the *Codex Exoniensis,* a tenth-century book of poetry held at Exeter Cathedral: 'What hangs at a man's thigh and wants to poke the hole that it's often poked before?' Answer: 'A key'. Somewhere in a pub in South London, somebody is probably telling a similar joke as you read this. Innuendo has always been essential to successful stand-up comedy.

This guide will fill in the history of stand-up comedy and furnish you with all the essential facts you need to convince your friends that you know your comedy onions. It may not turn you into an arena-filling comedian, but it will reveal what it takes to be one, and simultaneously demonstrate that there is in fact much more to modern stand-up comedy than innuendo. By the end of the book you will be able to hold your own in any conversation about comedy, and therefore minimise the risk of being rumbled as a bluffer. But be careful not to hold your own in public or you may be arrested.

TURNING A TRICK

In many respects stand-up comedy has hardly changed in the last thousand years. A man – and, sorry, it has generally been a man, although that is now changing as you will later see – attempts to make a group of people laugh with an infectious cocktail of wit, wisdom, and maybe some wordplay and charisma. He might even wear a funny hat and fall over. Some people will laugh at anything.

Money may well change hands at some stage – usually at the start of the evening. It has been noted that there is an interesting similarity between stand-up comedy gigs and prostitution. In both cases the 'punter' pays to have an emotional response in the company of someone they may not know personally and may never see again.

ROOTS AND RITES

Long before comedy became a part of show business, it was already part of our culture. Modern comedy has its roots in ancient pagan rites that some experts believe even predate Liverpudlian legend Ken Dodd telling his first gag about the Inland Revenue. It is remarkable how societies all over the world developed their own brand of humour which was both different and at the same time strikingly similar.

Native Americans, for example, believed in a comedic fertility character known as Kokopelli, a hunchbacked figure with a huge erection carrying a bag of seeds. Kokopelli would go around playing pranks on villagers, who would laugh so much that they would not notice him ravishing their women before moving on to another village the following night and doing the same thing. Maybe he was an ancestor of Russell Brand.

SEND IN THE CLOWNS

The clown has always had tacit permission to defy or simply ignore convention. In the Middle Ages jesters were able to speak their mind in the monarch's court. They were society's safety valve, a controlled way of expressing discontent. From Pueblo Indians mocking sacred ceremonies to a modern circus clown squirting water at the audience, comedy breaks down barriers. Stand-up Stewart Lee would start his 2005 show '90s Comedian by drawing a chalk circle on the stage to stand in. This, he explained, was what medieval clowns used to do outside churches to protect themselves from being persecuted for heresy.

By the 1800s a career in comedy was an established way of earning a living. The first great modern clown was Joseph Grimaldi, who was the Michael McIntyre of his day – careful not to offend, adored by the public, envied by his rivals. In *The Pantomime Life of Joseph Grimaldi*, author Andrew McConnell Stott recalls how one contemporary tried to besmirch Grimaldi's reputation for reliability by billing him in the line-up of a London show when he knew he was working in Birmingham. The clown got wind of the plot and after a breathless 100-mile, 19-hour journey by stagecoach made it onstage just in time.

Yet the strain of staying at the top took its toll, as it would do to many after him. Grimaldi suffered from depression and died in poverty and pain due to the damage caused to his body by his slapstick acrobatics. His legacy is the idea of the 'sad clown' who makes everyone laugh but goes home alone and cries himself to sleep. One should adopt an air of gravitas when talking of Grimaldi's fate, as a reminder that making people laugh is a serious business. Indeed, you might quote the great actor Edmund Kean who, on his deathbed, said: 'Dying is easy, comedy is hard.' Perhaps you might conceal an onion about your person and wipe away a convenient tear at this juncture.

MUSIC HALLS AND VAUDEVILLE

But this is comedy, and the bluffer should not dwell on the more morbid aspects of the profession. In the Victorian era, comedians were superstars, packing out music halls. You should demonstrate your inside knowledge by referring to Little Tich by his real name, Harry Relph. Tich was only four feet six inches tall and had six fingers on each hand. He was famous for his 'big-foot' dance in which he cavorted around in shoes that were two feet long. Tich would balance on them, strut around on them and even hide behind them. The bluffer must also mention Dan Leno, a man who entertained

Queen Victoria in her dotage and was given a diamond tiepin by King Edward and nicknamed the 'King's Jester'.

In the twentieth century vaudeville thrived. Cinema helped to make icons of the likes of Charlie Chaplin and Laurel and Hardy who had cut their teeth onstage. Later, George Formby was a household name, thanks to his gormless grin and suggestive songs such as 'With My Little Stick Of Blackpool Rock'. (Eat your heart out, Miley Cyrus.)

MAX MILLER

The first recognisably modern British comedian, however, was Max Miller. The Brighton-born entertainer was what was known as a 'front-of-cloth' comedian. He would stand in the footlights and fire out fusillades of jokes and stories while the curtain was down and the set rearranged for the next variety act. From the 1930s to the 1950s, Miller was a hugely popular household name, dominating live comedy. His outfits certainly made this stand-up stand out. Multicoloured brogues, plus fours (more usually seen on the golf course), kipper ties, trim silk jackets and tight-fitting trilbies made him look part travelling salesman, part circus clown. Miller was much loved by the public; if he was appearing in London and the show ran late, the guards at Victoria Station would hold the Brighton Express for him.

From the moment he strutted onstage, he was in full flow: 'Thank you very much, I expected more but I'm satisfied...' He would get plenty of material out of his outfits, running his hands over his hips and thighs: 'I've got new ones on tonight, all rubber. Do you wear them, lady? You do look funny when you take them off; you look like a golf ball.' Gradually he would build to a bawdy climax while discussing his recent hunt for seaside lodgings. 'I went to Blackpool and I went round looking for rooms… An old lady came to the door… I said could you accommodate me; she says I'm awfully sorry I'm full up. I said surely you could squeeze me in the little back room, couldn't you? She said I could but I haven't got time now.'

If Grimaldi created the 'sad-clown' legend, Miller added 'short arms, long pockets' to the modern comedian's psychological CV.

This 'saloon bar Priapus', as he was dubbed by playwright John Osborne, never actually swore. Everything was left to his audience's imagination. There was something delightfully conspiratorial about his act. In his most famous rapid-fire riff, he would pull out two joke books – one white book, one blue – and ask the audience which one they wanted: the clean white one or the dirty blue one. They invariably went for the blue book, knowing full well that that was where the rudest innuendos were. 'I don't care what I say, do I?'

If Grimaldi created the 'sad-clown' legend, Miller added 'short arms, long pockets' to the modern comedian's psychological CV. Miller had a reputation for being somewhat tight-fisted. Contemporaries joked that he was so mean that late in his career he was said to still have the first shilling he had ever earned. He was a past master at avoiding paying up when he lost a wager and was known to rush out of theatres straight after the curtain had come down without offering the band their traditional tip.

But as TV grew in popularity, Miller's days at the top were numbered. There was something about his Cheeky Chappie persona that did not translate to the new medium. The camera did not embrace him the way audiences did, or the way it would embrace Morecambe and Wise a decade later. It is hard to say exactly why Miller did not cross over onto the small screen. It was nothing to do with his act having to be tamed for TV, as some have suggested. Like Jimmy Carr or Frank Skinner today, Miller could be just as quick-witted without resorting to his 'blue book'.

Maybe he was just slightly too old. By the time TV came along as a major force, he was already in his fifties. Music hall was dying and he had nowhere else to go. He was keenly aware that he was the last of a certain breed: 'When I'm dead and gone, the game's finished,' he once said. And as far as music hall went, he was right. In 1958 he suffered a heart attack and, though he continued to perform, he took life more easily before going to the great gig in the sky in 1963.

STAGE TO SCREEN

Yet Miller paved the way for a generation of comedians who would become stars on TV as well as stage. Make sure you mention the lesser-known Arthur Haynes, who went from stage to screen, finding fame with his tramp character (his sidekick for a while was one of comedy's longest-serving straight men, Nicholas Parsons). Tony Hancock also went from live shows to sitcom fame, but everyone knows his tragic tale; Haynes will score you more points.

Light entertainment soon ruled the airwaves: Morecambe and Wise, Bob Monkhouse (who as a Dulwich College schoolboy would hang around by the stage door and try to sell jokes to Miller), Frankie Howerd and Tommy Cooper. And, lest we forget, there was also radio, with Spike Milligan and The Goons showing that comedy could be every bit as surreal as a Salvador Dali painting.

A generation made the leap from stage to screen. TV did not kill off stand-up; it brought it to a whole new audience. Comedy was a truly international phenomenon, from Lenny Bruce and Milton Berle in the USA to *Beyond The Fringe* in the UK featuring Peter Cook, Dudley Moore, Alan Bennett and Jonathan Miller.

1960s SATIRE

Comedy in the 1960s had a new confidence and irreverence. Old values were replaced. At Peter Cook's Establishment Club in Soho, jokes were made about royalty and prime minister Harold Macmillan, who was portrayed as a doddery old fool. Outrageous! Cook, who remains to this day the *sine qua non* of brilliant satirists, was his own tough act to follow. A dashing, handsome, sharp-witted superstar in the 1960s, he never lost his wit and ability. However, in the early 1970s he lost his direction, hosting a BBC chat show, *Where Do I Sit?*, which was so derided it was taken off the air mid-series and replaced by a new chat show hosted by a young journalist called Michael Parkinson. Whatever became of him?

THE ADVENT OF MODERN STAND-UP

But by the second half of the 1970s, comedy was in need of a revamp. *Monty Python's Flying Circus,* once so radical, had gone from being a late-night cult sketch show to a prime-time success, with John Cleese having an even greater hit with *Fawlty Towers.* And stand-up comedy was anything but cutting-edge. It was personified by the mother-in-law gags of the frilly-shirted, bow-tied brigade led by the likes of Bernard Manning, Frank Carson and Mike 'Wallop' Reid on Granada Television's quick-fire series *The Comedians.* The programme was cannily edited, fast with rapid cuts from gag to gag, so that viewers would not realise how wince-inducingly corny the acts really were in anything but the smallest of doses.

At the end of the decade, a change was in the air. A new stand-up revolution was brewing in the back streets of London's Soho. Truly modern comedy was about to be born. And it would have two fathers and no mother. How's that for modern?

WHAT'S THE ALTERNATIVE?

A life insurance salesman and a man who once opened for Cliff Richard walk into a bar… It doesn't sound like the start of a great gag, but Peter Rosengard and old-school comedian Don Ward are the two names you need to be *au fait* with when talking about the alternative comedy boom of the early 1980s. Without them, comedians would not be filling arenas and our TV screens today.

It was on a trip to Los Angeles in 1978 that Rosengard heard about a club called the Comedy Store. He had been looking at a house to buy in the Hollywood Hills and his real estate broker said he had to hurry away to do a stand-up gig. Fate, as it has an endearing habit of doing, had stepped in to change history.

Rosengard writes in his autobiography, *Talking to Strangers: The Adventures of a Life Insurance Salesman*, that he was intrigued and went to the small club himself where he laughed so much his family nearly had to cash in his own life policy. These were not stale old comedy hacks onstage but sharp, ambitious young gagmen doing tight 10-minute routines. Back in London, he decided to go to a similar comedy club but realised that there wasn't one. So he set one up himself. Looking around central London for a suitable property, he met Ward, who had a lease on an establishment called the Nell Gwynne Club in Soho.

This was a well-known striptease venue with a room going spare at weekends called the Gargoyle Club that had a fair bit of history. It had a mural by Matisse on the wall and the Prince of Wales – the future King Edward VIII – had been an occasional patron. It was here that Ward and Rosengard opened the Comedy Store on 19 April 1979. The posters advertising the club encapsulated the high-stakes thrills of stand-up: 'What's the difference between skydiving and appearing at the Comedy Store? Answer: In skydiving you can only die once.'

It is said that comedy is all about timing. Less than three weeks after the Store opened, Margaret Thatcher led the Conservative Party to victory in the general election. So not only was there a new 'alternative' comedy venue, now there was something for performers in the club to make jokes about. This was not the satire boom of the 1960s revisited. It was something much more visceral and angry that owed more to the recent punk-rock revolution than it did to Monty Python. There were few rules, other than Rosengard's insistence that the comedy should be non-racist and non-sexist.

ON THE BILL

All that was needed now were some comedians. Rosengard found a compère, Alexei Sayle, a furious surrealist-Marxist Liverpudlian who responded to an advertisement he placed in *Private Eye*. Slowly, a scene of sorts started to coalesce. Rik Mayall and Adrian Edmondson arrived from Manchester University as a comedy group called 20th Century Coyote (later to become the manic slapstick duo called The Dangerous Brothers). A famous early routine deconstructed the old gag: 'What's green and hairy and goes up and down? A gooseberry in a lift.' 'How did the gooseberry get in the lift?' they wanted to know (loudly).

♚

'What's the difference between skydiving and appearing at the Comedy Store? In skydiving you can only die once.'

Nigel Planer and Peter Richardson, contemporaries at drama college, also pitched up as The Outer Limits. In the mid-1970s they created a show mixing rock and comedy called Rank, about a rock festival raid by the police, in which Planer played a hippy called Neil. If you want to bluff about your in-depth knowledge of stand-up, you will need to know facts like this. Why? Read on.

It was right place, right time. Soho was starting to become fashionable, with the New Romantic movement setting risible and instantly forgettable sartorial trends. Walking down Old Compton Street, you might bump into Steve Strange dressed as a pirate at one end and Alexei Sayle in a tight-fitting mod suit and pork-pie hat at the other.

Sayle was paid £5 a night to link the acts and rant about Jean-Paul Sartre, Ford Cortinas and Lenin. A gong at the side of the stage was hit when acts had outstayed their welcome; one of the team couldn't find a flashing light to tell the acts when their time was up so picked up a small J Arthur Rank gong instead. Some acts were so dreadful that it was said even the bouncers heckled.

BEFORE THE BEGINNING

There were some notable precedents for what quickly became known as 'alternative comedy'. Two notable acts had swung open the door, and in any discussion about the birth of the genre, the bluffer should definitely name-drop Billy Connolly and Jasper Carrott, two natural storytellers who found their way into comedy in the mid-1970s via the folk-music circuit. But if you suggest that the absolute godfather of alternative comedy is Birmingham-born John Dowie, who did angry observational material before it became *de rigueur*, you will be on safe ground.

You should also mention a winner of the ATV talent show *New Faces* named Victoria Wood, who in 1978 took part in a topical revue called In At The Death at the Bush Theatre in West London. This was where the 25-year-old *ingénue* first had the opportunity to work with Julie Walters. Wood was never really part of the alternative comedy movement but, similarly disaffected with mainstream comedy, she was definitely moving in the same direction.

Another early bright spark was Keith Allen. He already had some showbiz experience – having been a stagehand at the Victoria Theatre and once strutting onstage naked while middle-of-the-road entertainer Max Bygraves was performing. The future father of chanteuse Lily Allen would go on to become a successful actor, author, singer-songwriter, TV presenter, artist, confrontational studio guest, and a few other things.

A NEW WAVE OF WAGS

Among the other unlikely acts who performed in the very early days was a young lawyer called Clive Anderson (who got into memorable trouble when the Bee Gees walked out of the chat show he was hosting) and a Denmark-born comedian called Sandi Toksvig. Simon McBurney, who went on to form arty-farty stage group Theatre De Complicite, also pitched up. Another class act from the very early days was Arnold Brown. He was a Scottish accountant but dreamed of being Finchley Road's answer to Woody Allen. 'I'm Scottish and Jewish – two racial stereotypes for the price of one.'

A growing number of women were also getting in on the act. Many, such as Jenny Lecoat, added a feminist agenda to their irreverent political humour. Pauline Melville used to satirise post-hippy cults: 'You know zen buddhists? The thin ones with anorexia nirvana…'

The Comedy Store did not exist in a vacuum, though. When displaying your extensive knowledge of alternative comedy's origins, be sure to mention other venues that offered a platform to this new wave of wags. Those who wish to appear well-versed in the history of alternative comedy must give other locations their due. The Elgin pub near Ladbroke Grove used to play host to cabaret events organised by subversive writer/comedian Tony Allen, who proved that anarchists can still organise things. Among his cadre of performers was Andy de la Tour, the brother of *Rising Damp*'s Frances de la Tour. Meanwhile over in South London, the Woolwich Tramshed – based in, who would have thought it, a former tramshed – used to run Fundation, featuring soon-to-be mainstream TV double act Hale and Pace. At one point Mayall and Edmondson worked on their act at the venue, too.

In Archway, North London, there was the Earth Exchange, which attracted a right-on audience and even some vegans if they had the energy to walk up the hill towards the entrance. You didn't have to wear jackets made out of muesli to be allowed in, but if you did you probably got a discount. Paul Merton, Harry Enfield, Rory Bremner and Jo Brand all played early gigs there before going on to TV. A couple of years after the Falklands War, there was an act called the Port Stanley Amateur Dramatic Society which was banned from the club because the routine involved throwing corned beef sandwiches into the audience.

AN ALTERNATIVE TO COMEDY?

As for the actual title of 'alternative comedy', Tony Allen has staked his claim to the term, having believed that his gigs were an 'alternative cabaret' and thus the comedians involved were 'alternative comedians'. According to his autobiography, *I Stole Freddie Mercury's Birthday Cake*, writer, comedian and South Londoner Malcolm Hardee appeared at gigs at the Ferry Inn, Salcombe, billed as 'Alternative Cabaret' in 1978 to differentiate them from the mainstream shows at the nearby yacht club. Maybe great minds think alike. Or perhaps it was something in the air. Most likely of all, maybe it was just a coincidence.

But the Comedy Store was the epicentre of the movement and Sayle was at the centre of the epicentre. Gradually, the Store evolved from something chaotic and unpredictable into something one might venture to call marketable. Performers were no longer ranting polemicists; they were also entertainers. Veteran comedian and host of TV's *Bullseye* Jim Bowen was not impressed. He sniffily dismissed alternative comedy an 'alternative to comedy'.

BOOM BOOM

So obviously Jim didn't agree that it was 'super, smashing, great', which was the closest he got to having a catchphrase. In those days, if you didn't have a catchphrase, you were at a serious professional disadvantage. Just ask Jim 'Nick Nick' Davidson or Jimmy 'Boom Boom' Tarbuck.

Yet the Comedy Store might have fizzled out. Except that one night, a young BBC producer named Paul Jackson was in the audience and liked what he saw. He persuaded his boss to let him make a programme showcasing this new generation. *Boom Boom... Out Go The Lights* was recorded on 16 May 1980 and featured Sayle, Keith Allen, Tony Allen, Mayall and Planer. The programme went out that October and had a very low audience appreciation index of 46 out of

100. But it was the point when the underground started to go overground.

Some of the acts decided to move on. In 1980, Peter Richardson opened the Comic Strip at the 200-seater Boulevard Theatre above another strip club, the Raymond Revue Bar in Walker's Court, a few streets away from the Store. The pick of the Store's young acts, most notably Sayle and 20th Century Coyote, and the not-so-young Arnold Brown, went with him.

MAGNET FOR MISFITS

They were joined by a new female double act. Dawn French and Jennifer Saunders met on a teaching course at the Central School of Speech and Drama. Their performances were largely staged for friends until Richardson pointed out that they might be able to make some money out of this comedy lark and they started to take things a little more seriously – or even frivolously.

But the Comedy Store remained a magnet for misfits who couldn't get a break elsewhere. Ben Elton was a nerdy, aspiring playwright who had known Mayall at Manchester University. Elton took a while to find his voice. Eventually he did, though some cynics said he sounded as if he had actually found Alexei Sayle's voice when he took over as compère in 1981. But there were differences. Sayle's rage had a surreal edge; Elton's anger was more grounded in mundane observational reality, trying to find the funny side of life's irritations, such as stepping in dog turds or trying to keep a double seat to oneself on the train. Critics might deride Elton today, but the bluffer should stand his or her ground and say that Elton was very much the Michael McIntyre (with attitude) of his day, touching a 'we've-all-been-there' nerve in his audience. His most recent sitcom *The Wright Way*, however, was widely and deservedly panned. While sticking up steadfastly for his early oeuvre, which included co-writing *Blackadder* with Richard Curtis, the bluffer should mention Elton's later output with a sorrowful shake of the head.

By the end of 1981 Ward was running the Comedy Store on his own. The original venue closed in December 1982 but the name lived on in various other Central London locations, eventually finding a home in a cosy basement in Oxendon Street between Leicester Square and Piccadilly Circus. It is still there today. You don't have to squeeze past strippers to get in.

ON THE BOX

Meanwhile, the early pioneers moved into TV and gradually became household names. It has been said that the rise of right-on alternative comedy prompted Thames Television to stop working with Benny Hill. The big breakthrough for the 'movement' came in 1982, when the BBC commissioned a series of *The Young Ones*. Mayall played fascist-hating student Rick; Edmondson reconfigured his stage character Adrian Dangerous, now called Vyvyan, with a Mohican and studded forehead; Planer played lentil-mental hippy Neil; and Richardson should have played Mike but dropped out and Christopher Ryan dropped in. The first series started on 9 November 1982.

While the others honed their comic personas on *The Young Ones*, Richardson, with time on his hands, met Jeremy Isaacs, the head of Channel 4 which was due to launch that autumn. This resulted in the *Comic Strip Presents* series, which pipped *The Young Ones* by starting on the night Channel 4 started, 2 November, with their spiffingly splendid Enid Blyton spoof, *Five Go Mad in Dorset*.

Rik Mayall died suddenly on 9 June 2014. The surviving core members (Richardson, Edmondson, French and Saunders) don't do much in the way of stand-up comedy any more but, 30 years on, some of the team still reconvenes between other projects to make *Comic Strip* films. Their logo – a cartoon atom bomb dropping on a patchwork quilt of English fields – effectively sums up the impact that their brand of alternative comedy had on the genre.

A NEW BOOM

Anyone claiming to be an expert in the origins and development of the new wave of comedy should point out that by the mid-1980s stand-up was seen as a viable career option – but not necessarily a particularly lucrative one. 'When I started, my ambition was to be at the sort of level of people I'd seen at Warwick Arts Centre,' said comedian Stewart Lee in 2013. 'In 1990 Newman and Baddiel did the Cochrane Theatre which held 400 people and I was thinking: "This has gone far enough, surely." Then three years later they were at Wembley..."

If you want to demonstrate that you understand how stand-up has evolved over the last three decades, latter-day *éminence grise* Lee puts it very well. Live stand-up comedy went from cottage industry to mainstream with remarkable speed. According to trade publication Pollstar, Michael McIntyre made £21 million in ticket sales from his *Showtime* tour in 2012. Not bad for someone who was scraping a living in 2005.

But in the mid-1980s, stand-up in the UK was still a more modest affair. In 1987 Ben Elton might have made a significant breakthrough when he played a record-breaking run at the 4,000-seater Hammersmith Odeon (now the Apollo), but there were other, much better-paid, old-school comedians still dominating stage and screen.

Signs were emerging, however, that their domination wouldn't continue for much longer. Other new acts were also beginning to make a big impact on the stand-up circuit.

THE POST-STORE GENERATION

Any comedy bluffer who wants to stand a chance of impressing in a conversation about the roots of the modern UK stand-up scene will have to be familiar with the following names: Sayle, Merton, Dee, Reeves and Mortimer, Newman and Baddiel, Skinner, and Kitson. These were the performers who really laid the groundwork for the foundations of the new comedy establishment.

Paul Merton, born in 1957, was another graduate of the post-Store generation. Merton was a comedy obsessive from an early age. While his schoolmates at the Jesuit-run Wimbledon College in South London had posters of Marc Bolan on their walls, he had pictures of Buster Keaton above his bed.

After leaving school he spent far too long working in the Tooting unemployment office. He had always wanted to be involved in professional comedy, but it was only after seeing Sayle perform that he saw it as a genuine career possibility. His first gig was at the Comedy Store in the spring of 1982, and from all accounts it went down pretty well. There was just one small problem. He was actually called Paul Martin and when he joined Equity it turned out that there already was an actor with that surname, so he changed his to the name of the London borough where he grew up.

— ♔ —

While his schoolmates had posters of Marc Bolan on their walls, Merton had pictures of Buster Keaton above his bed.

Merton has always specialised in a distinctive brand of surreal flights of fancy. One of his most famous early routines featured a policeman who is in court giving evidence about an incident during which he took hallucinogenic drugs: 'Thirty-five minutes later, I was sitting aboard an intergalactic spacecraft bound for the planet Zanussi, when I observed Constable Parish approaching me disguised as a fortnight's holiday in Benidorm.'

Just as Merton got his big break, however, he had another kind of break. In 1987 he broke his leg playing football at the Edinburgh Festival. He then contracted hepatitis A. Then he was about to record his first series for Channel 4 but had an adverse reaction to antimalarial tablets and ended up in the Maudsley psychiatric hospital in South London. He thought he was being followed by the Freemasons.

But things worked themselves out. By the early 1990s he was a household name, famous for his improvised skits on Channel 4's *Whose Line Is It Anyway?* and his freewheeling topical humour on BBC One's *Have I Got News For You*. As he told the *Daily Mail* in 2012: 'This don't half beat working in a dole office'.

DEE TIME

Another essential name to drop is **Jack Dee**. Born in 1961, he is another comedian whose life divides neatly into pre-Store and post-Store. Before Dee became a comedian, he had applied to drama school and even considered joining the Church of England priesthood. He eventually started working in the catering industry, managing a restaurant in Covent Garden.

The staff, many of them out-of-work actors, continually told him he had a talent for amusing people, so one night he decided to visit the nearby Comedy Store. It was an epiphany. 'I walked in and saw Jeremy Hardy, John Hegley and Paul Merton and I had this strongest feeling that they had started without me,' he later recalled. He decided to have a go, with some success, but that first gig started to look like a fluke when his happy-go-lucky persona failed to win the crowd over at later appearances.

Disillusioned, Dee decided to give up comedy after he had fulfilled his bookings. He was not so bothered about impressing the audience now and just went onstage as himself: sardonic, dry but – above all – glum. Suddenly the audience loved him. He had found his voice and he decided to stick at it. In 1991 he picked up a prestigious Perrier Award nomination at the Edinburgh Fringe Festival. Since then he has become a regular face on panel shows, in sitcoms and on tours. He even had a crack at straight drama, appearing onstage in the play *Art* and on TV in the crime thriller *Silent Witness*. He also won the very first series of *Celebrity Big Brother*. But he has always returned to stand-up. You would think that, after all this, Dee would have something to smile about.

A BIG NIGHT OUT

As the stand-up circuit grew, however, comedians were able to establish themselves without enduring a baptism of fire at the Comedy Store. In the mid-1980s in South East London, Darlington-born dandy Jim Moir renamed himself **Vic Reeves** to host a club night in Deptford when the original host pulled out. Moir briefly considered calling himself Craig Wildfowl, which begs the question: what's in a name? Could *Craig Wildfowl's Big Night Out* have been Channel 4's most popular comedy show in years?

Reeves hooked up with **Bob Mortimer**, a solicitor who was only too happy to take a break from court cases involving tenants with cockroach infestations. With the bespectacled Reeves bossing around the diminutive Mortimer, they resembled a post-punk Morecambe and Wise. Extra kudos will be earned by bluffers pointing out that, before they made it as a duo, Reeves appeared on Channel 4 music extravaganza *The Tube,* presenting a game-show segment entitled *Square Celebrities* – a parody of the ITV quiz *Celebrity Squares* – while swinging around on a wire.

Vic Reeves Big Night Out started on Channel 4 in May 1990. It baffled some, but was an immediate success among young viewers who appreciated the sheer lunacy of recurring characters. Bob played two seminal characters – dispenser of random punishments Judge Nutmeg and jobsworth pedant Graham Lister, who enjoyed nothing better than pushing a lump of lard through the eyes of a cardboard cut-out of Mickey Rourke.

Now that Reeves and Mortimer were a TV hit, they could embark on their first proper national tour. This coincided with their collaboration with Midlands popsters The Wonderstuff on the single 'Dizzy', which went to number one in 1991. The confident bluffer should now be well-equipped to argue convincingly that this was the moment when comedy became the new rock 'n' roll – and not when David Baddiel and Rob Newman played Wembley Arena in 1993.

After two series on Channel 4, Vic and Bob were poached by the BBC and, as well as making sketch shows, had a big hit with *Shooting Stars,* in which team captain Ulrika Jonsson had to grapple with a tray of vibrating sprouts. Vic and Bob are now seen as having had a huge influence on modern comedy, giving early breaks to the likes of Matt Lucas and David Walliams. You can't really imagine Craig Wildfowl casting such a large shadow over light entertainment.

FRANKLY SPEAKING

As shown by Paul Merton and Vic Reeves, a name change can work wonders. **Frank Skinner** was born Christopher Collins in West Bromwich in 1957, and it is easy to pinpoint his start in comedy. His twenties rattled by in a haze of no-future jobs, further education, punk gigs and heavy drinking. On his thirtieth birthday in 1987, he decided to give up the booze. The change of lifestyle gave him a handy safety net: 'If my career fails ,there's always alcoholism to fall back on,' he later reflected.

Skinner took a big – some would say reckless – risk and spent all of his savings booking an Edinburgh Festival venue before he even had a one-hour show. But compèring shows and doing new material every week sharpened his wits and, in 1991, the same year Jack Dee and Eddie Izzard also picked up nominations, he won the Perrier Award.

THAT'S YOU, THAT IS

David Baddiel and **Rob Newman**'s ascent was not quite as meteoric. Contemporaries at Cambridge, they both worked separately on the comedy circuit in the 1980s. By the turn of the decade, they had teamed up with fellow Cambridge graduates Hugh Dennis and Steve Punt for the radio and then TV series, *The Mary Whitehouse Experience*.

The TV series went out on BBC Two from 1990 to 1992 and gradually made stars of the performers. But there was a distinct split in the tone of the acts. While Punt and Dennis seemed straight and traditional (Punt had the dopey look of a young Eric Idle, and Dennis once worked as a marketing manager for Unilever), Newman and Baddiel had the hair and attitude of an indie band dreaming of John Peel discovering their demo tape.

The sketch that really captured the public imagination was 'History Today', in which Baddiel and Newman played two fusty academics who begin by having a serious discussion about history but end up trading puerile playground jibes, culminating in the catchphrase, 'That's you, that is'. The success of *The Mary Whitehouse Experience* was followed by Baddiel and Newman fronting their own series – *Newman and Baddiel in Pieces*. The 'History Today' professors returned, joined by further characters, most noticeably Newman's louche Jarvis, constantly on the prowl for young flesh.

Schoolchildren started quoting lines in the playground – the telltale sign that something is working. A tour was booked, dates sold out and more dates added. On 10 December 1993 the *Live and In Pieces* tour reached Wembley Arena. Comedy had graduated to another level of entertainment, and people who had not spotted Vic and Bob becoming pop stars started to talk about it as the new rock 'n' roll.

AN UNSTOPPABLE MOMENTUM

Throughout the 1990s and the early 2000s, comedy kept growing. Frank Skinner's show at Battersea Power Station in 1997 was the biggest ever solo gig in the UK. Eddie Izzard and Lee Evans started playing Wembley Arena. Comedy was moving into bigger spaces. New comedians kept emerging. Peter Kay was breaking through.

But before taking a closer look at arena stand-up comedy in the next chapter, it should be noted that size isn't everything. One comedian has defiantly done everything he can to stay away from the celebrity radar. He doesn't play rock venues or arenas, he doesn't employ a publicist or a manager. Yet ask any true fan of comedy who they admire and they will very quickly mention the name of **Daniel Kitson**.

The bespectacled, usually bearded, comedian, born in West Yorkshire in 1977, won the Perrier Award in 2002 but has since shied away from embracing the fame that goes with it. TV offers and interview requests are regularly turned down, resulting in *The Guardian* dubbing him the 'Salinger of stand-up'. As a teenager, Kitson was on the quiz show *Blockbusters,* where he said his ambition was to be a stand-up comedian. The clip was on YouTube for a while but at the time of writing, even those grainy few minutes have mysteriously disappeared. In fact, very little footage of him can be found online, though he did appear briefly as nerdy DJ Spencer 'for hire' in Peter's Kay's sitcom, *Phoenix Nights.*

Kitson's live shows swing between two extremes. On the one hand there are his theatrical monologues which have prompted theatre critics to compare him favourably to Alan Bennett. But catch him performing in a club or compèring a gig and he can be as crude as they come, as well as startlingly imaginative.

It is hard to understand why Kitson doesn't want to appear on screen – maybe because it dilutes profound and original material. But he really has to be seen live. If you haven't had the good fortune to see him, you should simply say that he is the most articulate, intelligent and talented stand-up of his generation. Anyone who has seen him will be unlikely to disagree.

Sachsgate prompted an unparalleled BBC moral clampdown. TV and radio comedy henceforth had to play safe.

NOBODY KNOWS ANYTHING

Screenwriter William Goldman famously said about moviemaking that 'nobody knows anything'. If he had been a comedy critic, he could have said the same about stand-up. Nobody could have predicted that by the end of the first decade of the new millennium, stand-up comedians would be regularly appearing in huge arenas as well as dominating the TV schedules.

There had undoubtedly been big comedy gigs before as previously mentioned, with Baddiel and Newman blazing a trail with the first UK arena show in 1993. Eddie Izzard, Lee Evans and Peter Kay would also be among the pioneers who moved comedy out of theatres and into venues more used to hosting rock gigs and sporting events. But after autumn 2008, arena comedy started to become a way of life. It would be the norm rather than the exception, the minimum requirement for any ambitious, talented stand-up with an ego that needed regular buffing. For a major comedian, filling an arena would be an essential part of the job description and not just something one dreamt about while sipping a post-gig digestif from a mucky beer mug backstage after a five-minute open mic slot.

Why so big? And why now? The answer to both questions is… the Sachsgate scandal. The following is a very short briefing for broad-minded bluffers. Send any delicate maiden aunts out of the drawing room first and read on for some essential bluffing knowledge.

FAWLTY JUDGMENT

Sachsgate started because the actor, comedian, sometime bohemian and broadcaster Russell Brand romanced a burlesque performer named Georgina Baillie, who, he then discovered, was the granddaughter of Andrew Sachs, who played Spanish waiter Manuel in *Fawlty Towers*. Comedy aficionado Brand was fascinated.

By a quirk of fate, Sachs was due to be interviewed on the telephone by Brand for his Radio 2 show shortly afterwards. When he didn't answer the call, Brand left answerphone messages in which Sachs was informed by Brand and his fellow broadcaster Jonathan Ross of the intimate dalliance in the crudest of terms. 'And so began perhaps the most significant minute of broadcasting in the BBC's history,' wrote Brand modestly in his autobiography, *My Booky Wook 2*.

The pre-recorded show was broadcast on 18 October 2008. Initially, only two complaints were made – and not about the particular content of the messages – but things quickly snowballed. MPs, including then prime minister Gordon Brown, criticised the two presenters, saying the messages were 'inappropriate and unacceptable'. Ross was suspended for 12 weeks without pay and Brand resigned. The BBC was fined £150,000, but the domino effect had only just started. Thereafter, comedy on the BBC would be monitored far more closely. Anything remotely controversial would have to be cleared before broadcast. Sachsgate prompted an unparalleled BBC moral clampdown. TV and radio comedy henceforth had to play safe.

CLEANING UP THE ACT

With Ross's BBC One chat show off the air, the corporation had to find a light-entertainment alternative, so they moved the stand-up series *Live at the Apollo* to the high-profile Friday slot. The first show, on 28 November 2008, featured someone who was the very antithesis of Russell Brand. Michael McIntyre was clean-cut, middle class and made trivial jokes about haircuts, choosing wine in restaurants and the domestic flotsam that men keep in their drawers.

Those 'man drawers' struck a chord. The country was in the icy grip of a recession and wanted easy laughs. New comedians were beamed into millions of homes on a Friday night. Little-known stand-ups suddenly had major exposure. Jason Manford and John Bishop were soon packing out 14,000-seat arenas. DVD sales went through the roof. Note that it is important to point out that Michael McIntyre would have been a star in any era, but the perfect storm was created to make him a superstar virtually overnight and boost the careers of those already toiling at the coalface.

NEW KINGS OF COMEDY

Alternative comedy had reached maturity, had a couple of kids and moved to the reassuring safety of the suburbs. Comedians looked like bank managers, albeit in slightly more expensive suits. So who were the new comedy kings?

Peter Kay was already a star before Sachsgate, but he's a lot bigger now. The affable Lancashire comedian was the first of a generation of comedians who specialised in simple, observational humour, inspired by working in a toilet-roll factory and behind the tills in the discount supermarket Netto. Kay's stories about his childhood seemed to resonate

> Alternative comedy had reached maturity, had a couple of kids and moved to the reassuring safety of the suburbs.

with the childhoods of everyone else in the country. It was the comedy of cobble-streeted, northern nostalgia, Proust meets *Coronation Street*. This was a universal world where your mum bought own-brand cola and snotty-nosed kids would slide around on their knees on the dance floor at weddings.

Kay's *Mum Wants A Bungalow* tour in 2002 established him as the ultimate comedy throwback. He was not sexist or racist or even offensive, but he was somehow so innately old-fashioned that it felt as if he had landed onstage direct from the year he was born in the early 1970s. His role in the

TV series *Phoenix Nights* effectively defined him. He played club promoter Brian Potter, whose variety acts, crooners and comedians were destined never to make it beyond the working men's club circuit. Impress your peers by pointing out that the first series was partly filmed at St Gregory's Social Club in Farnworth, the small town near Bolton where Kay was born.

ARENA GAMES

Lee Evans was born in Bristol but had moved to Essex as a boy, and is as intimately linked with that county as Kay is with Greater Manchester. The former boxer and 1993 Perrier Award winner has appeared in Hollywood films including *There's Something About Mary* and onstage in projects as diverse as Samuel Beckett's *Endgame* and Mel Brooks's *The Producers*. In 2002 he played at Wembley Arena and in 2005 he broke the record for a live show in the UK, playing to 10,108 people at the Manchester Arena.

In 2008 Evans announced that his *Big* tour would include a show at the O2 Arena. American comedy colossus Chris Rock beat him to it, but Evans's gig was still a landmark, proving that British comedians could perform in vast spaces. His 2011 *Roadrunner* tour then surpassed this earlier feat, with four nights at both Wembley and the O2. Bluffers should know that while this wasn't as many nights as Kay and McIntyre played on their last tours, it is not to be sniffed at.

APOLLO'S CHILDREN

Jason Manford has often been compared to Kay and there

are certain similarities, most notably a chatty, observational style with a penchant for product names that also harks back to Victoria Wood and Alan Bennett. Manford even did the same stand-up comedy module (yes, there are modules in comedy nowadays) as Kay at Salford University, but is now such a popular TV face in his own right that these comparisons aren't made quite so often.

John Bishop came to stand-up late. The Liverpudlian had a well-paid job in pharmaceutical marketing. Then one night in 2000 he decided to get onstage at Manchester comedy club Frog and Bucket's try-out night because it was £4 to get in but free if you did a turn. Bishop was an instant hit, entertaining the audience for half an hour by just chatting. He enjoyed it so much that he kept going back.

What he didn't realise was that one night, by coincidence, his wife Melanie, from whom he was separated at the time, happened to be in the audience and she saw a side of him that reminded her of the witty, easy-going, pre-marketing executive she had married. The pair were reconciled and Bishop found a new career – all by talking about his family and his life at home, from man-waxing to his spouse's Spanx underwear.

THE MAVERICKS

Many of these arena stars adopt a fairly straightforward comedy formula. They are likeable, working blokes. They are just like their audience, albeit richer and cleverer.

But there are a couple of arena-fillers who do not conform to this template in any way at all. One is Russell Brand, who, as noted earlier, was responsible for the recent growth of the whole arena comedy caboodle. The other is **Eddie Izzard**, who can reasonably claim to have kicked off the whole arena phenomenon a decade before. He doesn't fit into any obvious pigeonhole, which is why he's mentioned here.

For the first decade of his career, Izzard actively avoided appearing on TV, so if you wanted to see him you had to buy a ticket. Izzard certainly had plenty of live experience; he had been a street performer in Covent Garden before he found shelter in London's comedy clubs.

Born in Yemen in 1962, Izzard grew up in Wales and Northern Ireland. After an unpromising start on the comedy circuit in the early 1990s, everything seemed to slip into place. The storming gigs started to outnumber the catastrophic gigs. He moved from clubs to theatres. This coincided with his decision to reveal that he was a transvestite. Or 'action transvestite', to be more precise.

Izzard's particular brand of surrealist humour was hard to quantify. A little bit about history. 'I served in Vietnam… as a waiter.' A little bit about cake. A little bit about cats that weren't purring but 'drilling'. It looked improvised, full of erms and aahs, but although there was no written script – Izzard is dyslexic – there were set routines. When he got onstage, all of his ideas and theories about the world poured out of his mental blender. By the end of the 1990s, he was performing *Dress to Kill* at Wembley Arena in front of 10,000 fans.

Izzard has since pursued an acting career onstage and in the cinema, and in 2009 ran 43 marathons in 51 days for

Sport Relief. Now he is talking about a career in politics. He still returns to stand-up, of course, and did a few modest sell-out gigs at the O2 Arena in 2013. It would be perfectly reasonable for bluffers to say that he is comedy's ultimate renaissance man. And he is certainly one of the few British comics who can do a stand-up routine in French or German.

AND, NOT LEAST...

Former Billingsgate fish market porter **Micky Flanagan** has taken a more scenic route to stand-up success. At the start of the millennium, he was playing small clubs and was perfectly happy tinkering away. In 2007, at the age of 44, he became the oldest-ever Edinburgh Comedy Awards Best Newcomer nominee. Then suddenly, with the explosion in post-Sachsgate mainstream humour – 'just noticing things', as its denigrators would have it – Flanagan took off. It was his 'Out Out' routine that really cracked it for him. One minute you can be nipping out to the pub for a casual pint, then six hours later trying to get into a West End club in your slippers because you had never intended to go 'out' out in the first place. This was stand-up as social anthropology.

In 2013 at the ripe old age of 50, when others might have been pottering off down to their allotment, Flanagan went on tour with his new show, *Back In The Game*. A couple of dates at the O2 Arena became five dates, then six, then seven. There were also a few dates at Wembley Arena, and he had already played at the Hammersmith Apollo at the start of the tour. At the time of writing, Flanagan seems to be the stand-up with the most momentum.

Unless, that is, one is dropping the name of the man who started this whole game. In 2003 **Michael McIntyre** was reaching down the back of the sofa to find loose change to pay the bills. A decade later, the son of a gag writer who used to work with DJ-turned-comedian Kenny Everett is Britain's undisputed master of observational humour. (Bluffers might point out that another name for this is 'just noticing things that you find funny'.)

Critics will say that McIntyre doesn't do anything new. But you might point out that he, and many of his fellow TV stand-ups, do the old things better. If in doubt, you try standing onstage in front of millions of people and making them laugh by telling them about things you've noticed. And just think. If Andrew Sachs had been around to speak to Russell Brand on the radio, we might not have man drawers today and McIntyre's hand might still be down the back of the sofa.

At any one time there is probably
an episode of *Seinfeld* airing
somewhere in the world.
And if there isn't, there should be.

US AND THEM

An authoritative *Bluffer's Guide to Stand-up Comedy* would not be complete without a trip across the Atlantic – partly because some of the early American comedy superstars were actually British. Indeed, US comedy owes more to Limeys than just a shared language. Charlie Chaplin was born in Kennington, South London. Stan Laurel was born in Ulverston, Cumbria. And that master of the whiplash quip, Bob Hope, might have seemed as American as a wagon full of blueberry pie, but he was born in Eltham in the London borough of Greenwich. On his deathbed in 2003, at the age of 100, he was still quipping. When asked where he would like to be buried, Hope replied: 'Surprise me.'

WHAT'S NEW, PUSSYCAT?

But one of the greatest American comedians is barely considered worthy of a place in the pantheon of great stand-ups today because he has had such an illustrious film career. The assured bluffer, however, will drop the name, confident in the knowledge that **Woody Allen**, born Allen Stewart Konigsberg in the Bronx in 1935, was a working gagsmith long before he started to arrange the Oscars on his mantelpiece. As a child, he sold gags to other comedians, such as TV star Sid Caesar. It was only a matter of time before he cut out the middleman and went onstage himself.

In the early 1960s Allen started performing in clubs in Greenwich Village and soon developed his fast-talking, distinctively nervy style. His most famous routine, 'The Moose', told the story of how he shoots a moose but only stuns it, so decides to take it to a fancy costume party: 'The moose mingles… 12 o'clock comes – they give out prizes for the best costume of the night. First prize goes to the Berkowitzs, a married couple dressed as a moose.'

The moose is furious. A fight ensues, the two moose lock antlers and knock each other unconscious. Allen takes the moose, straps him to the bumper of his car, drives off and dumps him in the woods. Except that he has taken Mr and Mrs Berkowitz by mistake and the next day they are shot by hunters.

Allen had created a comedy persona that was instantly recognisable and one that would crop up regularly throughout his film career. By 1965 he was writing screenplays, most notably *What's New Pussycat?* starring Peter Sellers. He also wrote *Play It Again, Sam,* which was a Broadway hit and then a film, directed by Herbert Ross. But Allen wanted more control over his work and began directing his own films. *Sleeper, Annie Hall, Manhattan* and countless other classics – along with a few duds – followed.

Yet there is a twist to the tale worthy of an Allen stand-up routine. At the age of 77, he raised the possibility of doing stand-up again. In 2013, he told *Variety*: 'Mort Sahl is the guy who inspired me to go onstage for the first time in my life, and when I saw him the other night, I had that feeling again of, "I can do this". I thought, gee, it would be nice to get up there and do that again. It's a lot of work. You have to put together an hour of laugh, laugh, laugh, laugh. You can't dawdle.'

COMFY SWEATERS AND JFK

A surprising number of people might not be aware of **Mort Sahl**. This presents a perfect opportunity for comedy bluffers who will now know that he is an influential pioneer of satire in the USA. Sahl showed that there was a different way to talk onstage. Sahl, born in Canada in 1927, is considered by some to be the first comedian with a contemporary satirical approach. After serving in the US Air Force after the Second World War, he developed a new comedy style, picking up the day's newspapers and riffing on the stories in them. It might seem mundane now, but this kind of topical humour, particularly when it had a political edge, was startlingly radical at the time.

Sahl was famous for two things: his comfortable sweaters and his uncomfortable political humour. He once noted that 'Liberals feel unworthy of their possessions. Conservatives feel they deserve everything they've stolen.' But when JFK was assassinated in November 1963, Sahl became, some said, obsessed with the investigation, to the extent that he became a member of New Orleans District Attorney Jim Garrison's investigation team. Some also said that his obsession affected his work. People didn't want to go to comedy clubs to hear him talk about JFK. Although he drifted out of the spotlight, you'll be safe in saying that his influence clearly lives on.

SEVEN SHOCKING WORDS

A little after Sahl, another comedian cast a similarly large shadow over US comedy. **George Carlin**, born in 1937, also served in the US Air Force, but his anti-establishment stance was already much in evidence. He was labelled an 'unproductive airman' by his superiors and was court martialled three times before being discharged in 1957. Carlin looked conservative onstage in his suits and short cropped hair, but he was as radical as any of his contemporaries in the late 1960s. By the early 1970s, his image had caught up with his material. He even grew a beard, which stayed with him until his death in 2008.

Carlin was an outspoken stand-up, whose material dealt with what he called 'humanity's bullshit' such as war, rape and corruption. He was once arrested at a Lenny Bruce – more about him later – gig and in the 1970s he came up with his most famous routine, 'Seven Words You Can Never Say on Television'. You can probably guess most of them. Needless to say, Carlin didn't get the opportunity to repeat them on TV, but in July 1972 he did so at the Milwaukee Summerfest and was promptly charged with obscenity. The case was dismissed.

Carlin kept working throughout the subsequent decades and inspired younger comedians to push boundaries. Not always, though. In 2006 he appeared – or at least his voice did – in the Pixar film *Cars* in which he played Fillmore, a hippie-style psychedelic VW minibus with the number plate 51237 – his date of birth. We've all got to earn a buck.

HICKS COUNTRY

If comedy bluffers really want to impress their peers, however, they must drop the name of **Bill Hicks** into the conversation at the earliest opportunity. Hicks is widely regarded as the finest stand-up to emerge from America since Lenny Bruce (*see* page 71). He didn't just make people laugh; he also made them think.

Hicks was born in Georgia in 1961 but moved to Texas at an early age. He was brought up as a member of the Southern Baptist Church but soon started questioning his family's religious beliefs. His father would say that he

♕

Bill Hicks didn't just make people laugh; he also made them think.

believed that the Bible was literally true and the young Hicks would object: 'You know, some people believe that they're Napoleon. That's fine. Beliefs are neat. Cherish them, but don't share them like they're the truth.'

For a while he wanted to be a veterinary worker, but then he saw a stand-up performing on TV and resolved to make a living doing the same. When he was still a teenager, he would sneak out of the house at night to do gigs. By the time he was in his early twenties, Hicks was a familiar face as part of a group of comedians known as the Texas Outlaws, usually to be found enveloped in a cloud of cigarette smoke.

Hicks first toured the UK in 1990 and touched a nerve in England and at the Edinburgh Festival. Most comedians soften their edges as they get successful; Hicks got sharper and angrier. He condemned society, the government, religion, politics and consumerism. He even condemned himself. His damning critique of performers who were involved in advertising campaigns is regularly quoted: 'If you do an advert then you are off the artistic register forever.' A worrying number of comedians didn't listen – and still don't.

In October 1993 he was booked to appear on David Letterman's chat show. The recording seemed to go well and he had been allowed to do a passage about religion and 'the right to choose' which was potentially controversial. Then, when the programme was broadcast later that night, Hicks had been edited out. He was furious. Did Letterman cut it himself? Were the broadcasters leaned on by pro-life advertisers? In 2009 Letterman finally aired the routine and accepted responsibility for it being dropped.

It was a little late, though. Just over three months after the recording, in February 1994, Hicks died from cancer, aged 32. He hadn't mentioned that he was terminally ill in the Letterman interview.

BLACK HUMOUR

The best comedians don't just make you laugh; they have something to say. Like Hicks, **Richard Pryor** had plenty to talk about, but then he had had a colourful life – from growing up in a brothel to nearly dying when he set himself alight while freebasing cocaine. His in-concert movie *Live on the Sunset Strip* captures the black stand-up at the peak of his powers – relaxed yet sharp, angry yet philosophical, verbally on the money. His description and mime of having a heart attack is almost too painfully funny to watch.

Pryor, in turn, was a huge influence on **Chris Rock**. Both had issues with the N-word. Pryor used to pepper his set with it but then renounced it after a trip to Africa. Rock was already famous after appearing on *Saturday Night Live,* but he really made his name with one particular routine in the late 1990s contrasting 'niggas' and 'black people'. Rock rejected the view that a distorted image of African Americans had been deliberately cultivated by the US media. In his routine, he says: 'When I go to the money machine tonight, alright, I ain't looking over my back for the media, I'm looking for niggas!'

WHAT'S THE DEAL WITH...?

Scabrous humour lives on in the USA in the form of **Louis CK**, a Mexican-American whose routines are not explicitly political but have a more subtle philosophical agenda. But what the USA has become particularly good at is producing slick, efficient comedians who simply make you laugh. They are the American equivalent of the British 'noticing brigade'. But in the American vernacular it's more 'What's the deal with…?' One comedian in particular has taken this brand of observational humour and turned it into an art form.

Jerry Seinfeld started out as a stand-up soon after graduating from Queen's College in his home town of New York with a degree in communications and theatre. He had some success very quickly and in 1979 even had a small part in the sitcom *Benson* as Frankie, a courier who had comedy routines that no one wanted to hear: 'Do you know what Custer's last words were? Does anyone here speak Indian?'

In 1988 he created *The Seinfeld Chronicles* with fellow stand-up Larry David, in which he played a stand-up comedian coincidentally called Jerry Seinfeld. The show – famously said to be 'about nothing' – changed its title to *Seinfeld* (show your depth of TV trivia by pointing out that there was already another show called *The Marshall Chronicles*) and went on to be one of the most successful sitcoms of all time, running until 1998. At any one time there is probably an episode of this masterful sitcom airing somewhere in the world. And if there isn't, there should be.

When the show ended, however, Seinfeld went back to stand-up comedy, effectively starting again from scratch. He continues to perform live as well as to collect ridiculously expensive vintage cars and make TV shows. He certainly doesn't need to work for a living. Thanks to syndication deals, it has been said that Seinfeld has earned over $800 million. A comedy about nothing has more than proved that it is worth something.

FUNNY WOMEN

This should not come as a surprise, but women are funny. Indeed, they have been funny for many years. In 2013 **Bridget Christie** won the Foster's Edinburgh Comedy Award, confirming, in case anyone still doubted it, that women are funny. Others to pick up Edinburgh's top gong include Jenny Eclair in 1995 and Laura Solon in 2005. But should anyone dare to challenge the bluffer about the place of women in comedy, here are a few persuasive examples of female stand-ups with a full skeleton of funny bones to set the record straight.

Joan Rivers is now in her early eighties – though, thanks to cosmetic surgery, some bits are substantially younger. She has been a figurehead for women's comedy for over five decades. Her face may have changed over the years but her material remains stiletto-sharp. Born Joan Alexandra Molinsky, she specialises in an abrasive, brash, typically New York kind of humour – aggressive yet with a self-deprecating streak as wide as the Hudson River. Like many American comedians she got her big TV break on the *Tonight Show* in 1965, where she wowed both the audience and host Johnny Carson.

In 1987 Rivers suffered a personal tragedy. Her husband, Edgar Rosenberg, committed suicide. Rivers dealt with the situation in the way she knew best – making jokes about it. She later recalled how she coped with the subject with her daughter Melissa when they went out to dinner. 'I looked at

Not so much a comedian as an unstoppable force of nature, Joan Rivers will probably still be gigging when she's 100.

the prices on the menu and I said, "Melissa, if Daddy was alive he'd kill himself all over again."' Rivers was more self-deprecating than ever. 'My husband killed himself. And it was my fault. We were making love and I took the bag off my head.'

No taboo is left unbusted – from haemorrhoids to the Holocaust, she goes for it. Not so much a comedian as an unstoppable force of nature, she'll probably still be gigging when she's 100. If you pretend to know anything about comedy, you will say she is one of the best of all time.

NUT FARM

Roseanne Barr is another larger-than-life comedy colossus who went from stand-up fame to fronting her self-named hit sitcom *Roseanne* from 1988 to 1997. Her sitcom character, Roseanne Conner, was not a million miles away from her tough, working-class 'domestic goddess' stand-up persona. Barr had the kind of complicated upbringing that provided the perfect comedy apprenticeship. She had a Jewish background, but grew up in Salt Lake City where her parents were also involved in the Church of Jesus Christ of Latterday Saints. She once said: 'Friday, Saturday, and Sunday morning I was a Jew; Sunday afternoon, Tuesday afternoon and Wednesday afternoon we were Mormons.'

She is controversial as well as comic. In 1990 Barr sang the 'Star-Spangled Banner' at a baseball game between the San Diego Padres and the Cincinnati Reds and was said to be 'screechy', bringing a whole new meaning to the phrase 'extraordinary rendition'. Barr said she had been having trouble hearing herself over the public address system so sang as loudly as possible.

This did not explain why she also grabbed her crotch and spat on the ground after she finished singing. She said she had been asked by officials to 'bring humour' to the song but it didn't stop president George Bush Sr from calling her performance 'disgraceful'. Roseanne's reputation for being unpredictable lives on; in 2011 she fronted *Roseanne's Nuts,* a TV show about her macadamia nut farm in Hawaii.

The coolest American female stand-up around, however, is **Sarah Silverman,** whose comedy tends to focus on the darker side of life. Silverman makes even Rivers seem a little tame. Children will recognise her as the grumpy girlfriend in *School of Rock,* but she is best known in comedy circles for gags such as: 'I was raped by a doctor… which is so bittersweet for a Jewish girl.'

JOLLY HOCKEY STICKS

By comparison, over on this side of the Atlantic, female stand-ups tend to be relatively demure. A worthy inheritor of the sort of wry British humour exemplified by the uniquely brilliant Joyce Grenfell in the 1950s and 1960s is **Victoria Wood**, although she added a distinctively less posh twang. The Prestwich-born comedian didn't rise via the traditional route of comedy clubs; instead, she came up via the *Britain's Got Talent* of the 1970s, ITV's *New Faces,* which she won in 1973. Her career took a rather strange direction, however, when she landed a regular slot on the popular consumer programme *That's Life!*, where she performed topical songs between pictures of phallic carrots and ducks on skateboards, and poems about incompetent town councils.

Wood was a contemporary of the alternative comedy scene but was never a part of it. What she had in common with its early exponents was a rejection of old-school sexist, racist Benny Hill-style comedy. Wood's wit was more rooted in gossipy northern musical-hall humour and references to Gypsy Creams and Garibaldis. She ploughed her own parallel furrow which led to BAFTAs and record-breaking runs at the Royal Albert Hall. Health issues did not hold her back; in fact, they gave her material. When she was in her forties, doctors found a twisted fibroid growth in her womb and had to operate. Her response onstage at the Royal Albert Hall in 2002 was: 'Fibroids? Isn't that a breakfast cereal?'

For the last decade, Wood has talked about retiring from stand-up comedy and has worked more on other projects – writing the musical version of *Acorn Antiques* and a TV drama about the early life of Eric Morecambe (in which she played his mum and Vic Reeves played his dad – a role Reeves was always destined to play). But she keeps coming back to stand-up. In 2010 she compèred an all-female benefit gig for Angina Awareness at the Theatre Royal in London's Haymarket and noted how far women in comedy had come; two decades earlier, she pointed out, it would have just been Wood, Jo Brand and Danny La Rue on the bill.

BRAND BANTER

Jo Brand may be close to being a national treasure (application pending) but this was not always the case. She cut her teeth playing the roughest pubs and clubs in the 1980s. Not that this bothered her. She had seen far worse as a psychiatric nurse: dysfunctional families, paranoid schizophrenics, a large naked man sitting on the floor with matches between his toes during therapy sessions, while another patient sang 'Oh What a Beautiful Morning'.

Brand was born in 1957 in Sussex and grew up in Kent. She left home at 17, staying on at school part-time to do her A levels, eventually pursuing a career in nursing. But in 1986 she decided that she would like to try stand-up. She hurtled through her five minutes anaesthetised by alcohol and decided she liked it. At first she did gags about Freud, but they didn't go down too well. When she started to do gags about herself and her weight, things clicked: 'I went to a health farm. Ended up eating my bedroom.'

For a while she continued to work as a psychiatric nurse

in South London, but her two worlds were starting to collide. At a show at the Institute of Contemporary Arts, a naked man was talking into an early mobile phone. Other people thought he was an art installation and left him to it; Brand recognised him as a previous patient. Eventually, in the late 1980s, Brand quit the wards to take on the greater madness of comedy full-time and has not looked back.

There have, of course, been other female triumphs. Bluffers should ensure that they name-drop the aforementioned motormouth Jenny Eclair, who was the first female comedian to win what was then the Perrier Award with a solo show in 1995. True lovers of important comedy minutiae should, however, point out that Emma Thompson won the very first Perrier in 1981 as part of the Cambridge Footlights, along with Stephen Fry, Hugh Laurie, Tony Slattery, Penny Dwyer and Paul Shearer. More recently, Sarah Millican has joined the ranks of leading female stand-ups.

FALLING OVER LAUGHING

And then there is **Miranda Hart,** who is proof that if at first you don't succeed, just stick to it. And if you fall over, just get up and fall over again. Hart – whose father David Hart Dyke CBE LVO RN was the captain of HMS Coventry, which was sunk during the Falklands War in 1982 – was educated at posh Downe House in Berkshire. Hart had an interest in comedy from an early age and regularly took character-based shows up to the Edinburgh Festival, but for a while it looked like she might also sink.

A lead role in the 2006 sci-fi sitcom *Hyperdrive* failed to kick-start her career, though a supporting role as a cleaner in Lee Mack's comedy *Not Going Out* in 2009 gave her some traction. But just as it looked as if Hart was never going to make it beyond second fiddle, she was commissioned to write and star in a BBC Two sitcom, *Miranda* (which started life on Radio 4 as *Miranda Hart's Joke Shop*).

Hart has single-handedly made falling over funny again for the first time since the heyday of Norman Wisdom. She has also found the time to write a book and appear in a straight role in the TV drama *Call The Midwife* as Camilla 'Chummy' Fortescue-Cholmeley-Browne. Hart is clearly a woman of many talents. It is less well known that she once had a trial for Queens Park Rangers ladies' football team.

All of which is confirmation, as if it was needed, that despite the claims of unreconstructed male chauvinists, women are funny. If anyone tells you otherwise, then simply recite the names mentioned above. Hart, Brand and Wood might sound like a firm of solicitors but if you are not laughing at them, please check your pulse at the earliest opportunity because you might be dead.

'It's not that I'm afraid to die, I just don't want to be there when it happens.'

Woody Allen

GAGGING FOR IT

I t is the hardest type of humour in the world, yet the one-line gag seems like the simplest. While some of the world's greatest comedians tell lengthy stories, spin yarns, fly off at surreal tangents or try to bring the government down, a certain type of stand-up goes straight for the funny bone.

Bluffers holding court should assert boldly that one of the best one-liner merchants of the modern era was **Bob Hope**. His gags entertained Americans from the vaudeville era until his death in 2003. Hope was never short of a pithy wisecrack – partly because he had a team of writers constantly churning them out for him. He paid well, but made them work for it; he was infamous for his habit of calling writers in the middle of the night and demanding 'Thrill me' down the phone.

The British TV compère and entertainer Bob Monkhouse once wrote for Hope and recalled excusing himself during a meeting only to be informed that it was not time for a break. 'He knocked on the door and called out: "There's paper in there, keep writing."'

Another master of the one-liner was **Woody Allen,** who

added a more philosophical twist to his gags. If he wasn't musing on the meaning of life, he was reflecting about how mean people had been to him. On a good day he combined both themes:

I'm very proud of my gold pocket watch. My grandfather, on his deathbed, sold me this watch.

What if everything is an illusion and nothing exists? In that case I definitely overpaid for my carpet.

It's not that I'm afraid to die, I just don't want to be there when it happens.

Allen was inspired by, among others, **Groucho Marx**, who certainly knew how to deliver a gag for maximum comic effect – back bent, eyes bulging, cigar in hand. The following are a selection of choice Marx cuts, some worthy of Oscar Wilde, who is not otherwise included in these pages. He never played the late show at the Comedy Store.

Room service? Send up a larger room.

Those are my principles. If you don't like them, I have others.

I never forget a face but in your case I'd be glad to make an exception.

Another estimable Jewish-American gagmeister is **Jackie Mason,** still performing his one-man show more than half a century after his first performance. His classic, definitive deadpan delivery has been a huge influence on comedians on both sides of the Atlantic. One can see echoes of his astute observational humour in Jerry Seinfeld and his cosmic grumpiness in someone like Jack Dee, and the Wisconsin-born former rabbi is still packing 'em in with some classic wordplays like:

Did you know that the Jews invented sushi? That's right - two Jews bought a restaurant with no kitchen.

I have enough money to last me the rest of my life unless I buy something.

It's no longer a question of staying healthy. It's a question of finding a sickness you like.

The great British visual comedian **Tommy Cooper** was a prolific source of one-liners, with which he used to intersperse with his (usually unsuccessful) tricks:

I'm on a whisky diet. I've lost three days already.

I sleep like a baby... I wake up screaming every morning around 3am.

I said to the doctor, 'It hurts when I do this' [raises arm]. He said, 'Well, don't do it.'

Any bluffer quoting Cooper, however, has to proceed with caution. A few years ago, quick-fire comedian Tim Vine discovered that a number of his gags were appearing on websites and being credited to Tommy Cooper. Not that Cooper can be blamed – he died well before the Internet took off.

Every year since 2008, the TV channel Dave has carried

out a search for the funniest joke of the Edinburgh Fringe. Vine is usually nominated and it is frankly scandalous that he has only won the award once, in 2010. In 2013, for instance, he only came fourth with 'My friend told me he was going to a fancy dress party as an Italian island. I said to him, "Don't be Sicily."' In the interests of balance, it

---

♔

> 'You know who really gives kids a
> bad name? Posh and Becks.'
>
> *Stewart Francis*

---

should also be pointed out that he was a contender in 2013 for worst joke of the Fringe for 'I once did a gig in a zoo. I was babooned off.'

Here is a rundown of Dave's winners:

2013: Rob Auton
'I heard a rumour that Cadbury is bringing out an oriental chocolate bar. Could be a Chinese Wispa.'

2012: Stewart Francis
'You know who really gives kids a bad name? Posh and Becks.'

2011: Nick Helm
'I needed a password eight characters long so I picked Snow White and the Seven Dwarves.'

2010: Tim Vine

'I've just been on a once-in-a-lifetime holiday. I'll tell you what, never again.'

2009: Dan Antopolski

'Hedgehogs. Why can't they just share the hedge?'

2008: Zoe Lyons

'I can't believe Amy Winehouse self-harms. She's so irritating she must be able to find someone to do it for her.'

There is one major omission here. **Milton Jones,** a purveyor of prime cuts of concentrated comedy, has never won this accolade. Sometimes these lines are long, but take a deep breath and they still count as one-liners. Here are some of his choicer morsels:

Years ago I used to supply filofaxes for the mafia. Yes, I was involved in very organised crime.

Recently I've been attending meetings of Eavesdroppers Anonymous – not that they know!

My grandfather is always saying that in the old days people could leave their back doors open. Which is probably why his submarine sank.

Don't believe anyone who tells you that comedians are not competitive. Jimmy Carr likes to go further than just come up with one-liners. He set himself the challenge of coming up with the shortest joke in the world. Tim Vine had a five-word one: 'Velcro. What a rip off.' But Carr beats those five words with a two-word gag that is diminutive in every sense: 'Dwarf shortage.'

As these less-is-more examples have amply demonstrated, there is a real craft to writing a one-liner. Often they are done by a kind of verbal reverse engineering. A comedian will notice a word or a phrase that can have an alternative meaning and then work backwards to come up with the set-up that will turn the phrase into a joke. Take this example of backwards thinking, Vine-style: 'Did you know if you chop a horse in two then bang the halves together, it sounds like someone riding a coconut?' But a word of warning to any bluffers interested in deconstructing jokes: it is not as easy as it looks. It was once said that analysing comedy is like dissecting a frog. Nobody laughs and the frog dies.

Americans seem to be very good at one-liners. **Steve Martin** used to specialise in offbeat gags. 'Boy, those French: they have a different word for everything!' On the same theme, a certain George W Bush is reputed to have once said: 'The problem with the French is that they have no word for entrepreneur' (although, sadly, it wasn't meant as a joke).

For many comedians, one-liners are a way of landing spots on those all-important American chat shows when you only have a few minutes to make an impact. One-liners are the SAS of comedy; they get in quickly, do the job and get out again before you have even noticed.

Steven Wright, the frizzy-haired writer and comedian, broke through in the early 1980s with a bottomless pit of understated absurdism delivered in a deadpan monotone.

'You never know what you have until it's gone, and I wanted to know what I had, so I got rid of everything.' Wright heavily influenced the next generation of American stand-ups.

The coolest name to drop if talking about one-liners is American cult hero **Mitch Hedberg,** who never performed in England and died in 2005, aged 37. Hedberg's jokes had an almost zen-like quality to them that perfectly complemented his long-haired stoner sensibility: 'The depressing thing about tennis is that no matter how good I get, I'll never be as good as a wall.' Or, 'I find that a duck's opinion of me is largely influenced by whether or not I have bread.'

They were verbal double takes, where you had to take a moment to get it: 'One time, this guy handed me a picture of him, he said, "Here's a picture of me when I was younger." Every picture is of you when you were younger.'

Emo Philips is also fond of messing with multiple meanings: 'I like going to the park and watching the children run around because they don't know I'm using blanks.' His dark, warped gags, paired with his floppy, asymmetrical hairstyle, sent the needle shooting off the offbeat register. His world view was as lopsided as his fringe: 'When I was 10, my family moved to Downers Grove, Illinois. When I was 12, I found them.'

Anyone who says that comedians doing one-liners are dull and repetitive should be pointed immediately in the direction of **Demetri Martin.** He sometimes illustrates his gags with drawings; sometimes he plays the guitar while he talks. Martin is obsessed with word games so it is no surprise that he loves one-liners. His 2003 Edinburgh debut, which won the Perrier Award, was called *If I* – not only was the show title a palindrome but the show included a frankly epic 224-word palindrome, entitled 'Dammit I'm Mad'.

Martin constantly finds new meanings in ordinary phrases:

> *I heard this lady say: 'I love kids.' That's nice…little weird, though…it's like saying: 'I like people for a little while.'*

> *I was on the street and I saw this guy wave to me. He came up to me and said: 'I'm sorry, I thought you were someone else.' I said: 'I am.'*

One-liners work best if you want to get as many laughs as possible in a limited time. Which, to be truthful, is ultimately the aim of all stand-up comedy. *Guinness World Records* includes the record for the most jokes told in an hour. At the time of writing, the record is held by an Australian comedian called Anthony 'Lehmo' Lehmann, who told 549 jokes in one hour at the Rhino Room Club, Adelaide, South Australia, in 2005. Tim Vine had previously held the record, telling 499 jokes in an hour.*

With the advent of Twitter, of course, where brevity is crucial, one-liners have taken on a whole new relevance. Gags that can be told in fewer than 140 characters can instantly fly around the world. You don't need to go out

---

*Stop press: the record has been taken away from Lehmo and returned to Vine. According to website Chortle, Lehmo had breached guidelines. On hearing the good news, Vine said: 'I'm going to crack open some champagne. Actually that's a bit dangerous. Perhaps I'll just remove the cork.'

gigging (unless you want to get paid). Social media has made a star out of American comedian **Rob Delaney,** who won the Funniest Person on Twitter Award in 2012. Delaney was already a professional stand-up, but Twitter pushed him to another level. On Twitter, Delaney has a reputation for clever one-liners, though onstage he does tell longer, more complex stories. He recently tweeted: 'Peter Jackson just found a postcard JRR Tolkien wrote his nephew in 1938. He's turning it into 22 nine-hour films.'

Maybe it should be left to another (unrelated) Delaney, the prolific British one-liner specialist **Gary Delaney,** to have the last word with a classic one-liner: 'As a kid I was made to walk the plank. We couldn't afford a dog.'

'Do you enjoy wearing women's clothing?' Lenny Bruce was asked. 'Sometimes.' 'When is that?' 'When they fit.'

LORDS OF MISRULE

Lenny Bruce, born Leonard Alfred Schneider in 1925 in Mineola, New York, was already causing trouble long before he was making people laugh. At school he used to steal other kids' lunches. During the Second World War he joined the US Navy. When the war was over, he claimed that he was a transvestite so that he could get discharged. 'Do you enjoy wearing women's clothing?' he was asked. 'Sometimes.' 'When is that?' 'When they fit.'

Lenny Bruce is the first name bluffers should drop when it comes to discussing comedians behaving badly. He was a drug addict offstage and said the unsayable onstage. Bruce wanted to expose the hypocrisy of a society that allowed segregation depending on the colour of a person's skin but got upset about four-letter words. He was the epitome of comedy cool. Others wore suits; Bruce wore a denim jacket and jeans or a chic Nehru jacket. (Don't forget that this was an unusual look in the 1950s.) His hit album, *The Sick Humor of Lenny Bruce,* released in 1959, caught him in full, ferocious flight, imagining Hitler in show business and the Catholic Church running itself as a criminal organisation.

In September 1961 police found 36 ampules of methedrine along with syringes in his hotel room. In court his defence argued that nothing had been found that matched what was on the search-and-seizure warrant and the case was dropped. But his problems were only starting.

OBSCENE AND HEARD

Bruce was arrested for obscenity in October of the same year at the Jazz Workshop in San Francisco for using a word commonly used to describe someone who performs an intimate oral sex act on the male sexual organ. Bluffers would never stoop to repeat it (well, not in civilised company, anyway).

His defence team argued that he was merely following in the satirical tradition of Jonathan Swift, Rabelais and Aristophanes. He aimed to show that words contained no essential harm but had a pejorative meaning imposed on them. He was found not guilty of violating Section 311.6 of the Penal Code of the State of California. However, from this point on his performances would be monitored.

In 1962 he was a sensation at Peter Cook's Establishment Club in London. Bruce moved into Cook's Battersea flat and his host asked if there was anything he needed. Bruce wanted some drugs. Cook thought that his comedy partner Dudley Moore might be able to help because he moved in jazz circles and knew some of the hepcats, but Dud couldn't get anything stronger than aspirin. Luckily, Bruce then decided that he wanted chocolate cake instead – much easier to score in SW11.

Back in the USA, Bruce was constantly scrutinised. At one show there was even a policeman who was fluent in Yiddish in case he decided to be obscene in a different language. In March 1964 he was arrested twice in the same week. But as a sophisticated bluffer you should say that, despite his tiresome obsession with using obscenities as part of his act, you are nonetheless a fan (as were Bob Dylan, Jonathan Miller, Woody Allen, Arthur Miller, Richard Burton and Paul Newman).

Despite the liberal intelligentsia sticking up for him, Bruce was found guilty of obscenity and sentenced to four months in jail. But in March 1965, while free on appeal, he fell out of a hotel window and suffered multiple fractures to his ankles and hip. He died in August 1966. He was found with a needle in his arm, having fallen off the toilet seat. Record producer Phil Spector said that Lenny died of 'an overdose of police.' Bruce was gone but his influence for taboo-destroying behaviour certainly outlived him.

BRAND X

In April 1990 Russell Brand's PE teacher wrote a report on his errant pupil at Grays School in Essex: 'Sometimes he gives the impression that rules do not apply to him.' The future comedy star was 14, but was already exhibiting traits that would land him in rehab, in multiple beds, in fights and in headlines, all of which would help to create a truly unique performer.

Like Bruce, Brand showed a precocious disregard for convention. As a teenager he landed a place at the Drama

Centre in Chalk Farm. He drank heavily, used drugs recklessly, slept around and for a while had a mouse called Elvis living in his hair. Eventually he was expelled. The mouse stayed on, graduated and is currently at the RSC.

Brand decided to concentrate on stand-up and was determined to be different, sometimes by throwing bits of dead animals into the audience. The idea was to make people think, but he usually just ended up irritating them. In early 2000 he reached the final of the Hackney Empire New Act of the Year competition. Previous finalists included David Baddiel, Eddie Izzard, Harry Hill and Harry Enfield. He failed to win.

♛

Russell Brand's edit button was still not fully functioning. At the Video Music Awards he called President George W Bush a 'retarded cowboy fella'.

He did get noticed, however, and TV work started to come in, but it failed to curb his enthusiasm for anarchic behaviour. The day after the 2001 Twin Towers tragedy, Brand turned up at MTV with his drug dealer. He had also, incidentally, decided to come into work wearing a camouflage combat jacket, a false beard and a tea towel on his head, doing a passable impersonation of Osama bin Laden. He was sacked shortly after.

Not even Bruce at his most wayward behaved like this. But there is a happy ending to this tale. Brand acquired a new agent, checked into rehab and became a reborn Russell Brand. His edit button was still not fully functioning, though. At the Video Music Awards in 2008 he called President George W Bush a 'retarded cowboy fella'. It helped to make his name in the USA but he decided to keep a low profile for a while, just doing his Radio 2 show and occasionally getting his friend Jonathan Ross in as a guest.

As the observant bluffer will now be aware, Sachsgate changed British stand-up. Brand moved on. There were more films, including *The Tempest* with Helen Mirren, marriage to singer Katy Perry and, more recently, the small matter of calling for a rethink of the way the country is run. His last tour was called *Messiah Complex*. There are no half measures where Brand is concerned.

THE REAL LORD OF MISRULE

Yet while the novice bluffer might cite Brand and Bruce as comedy's premier upstarts, the audacious bluffer will hark back much further into comedy history to impress their friends. Russell and Lenny are mere pussycats compared to **Frank Randle,** music hall's ultimate Lord of Misrule.

Randle was born in Aspull, Lancashire, in 1901. He worked as an acrobat and solo stand-up before fronting his own touring company, Randle's Scandals, which later featured Roy Castle, future host of the TV show *Record Breakers*. During the Second World War, Randle's movies were huge money-spinners, constantly breaking box-office records.

So far, so normal. Offstage, Randle appeared to be a distinguished sort of chap, but he had had his teeth removed, which meant he could use different sets of dentures for each character he created onstage, from a pipe-smoking old boatman to his most famous creation, the drunk hitchhiker, complete with catchphrase, 'I've supped some stuff tonight.'

He was known to hurl his false teeth at hecklers, but offstage he was monstrous, making little effort to get on with people. He once locked four-feet-one-inch singer/dancer Sadie Corré in her dressing room without any clothes, and another time chased her with a loaded Luger. He also fired at an extra during a film shoot. He would smash up his dressing room with an axe if he was in a bad mood or throw empty beer bottles at mirrors. He set fire to a hotel when he was unhappy with room service, and when not performing he would disappear on three-day benders. When sharing a bill with superstar rival George Formby, he trapped him in a lift backstage and went to the pub.

His most famous stunt involved hiring an aeroplane and bombarding Blackpool with toilet rolls after he had been convicted of obscenity. There is some dispute over whether this incident actually happened; some say Randle bombed Accrington by mistake.

It was not his bad behaviour that finished him off, though; it was the box. A new generation of TV-friendly comedians was emerging and variety was starting to die. Tuberculosis and beer compounded Randle's problems. By the mid-1950s he was being chased for unpaid tax and in 1955 was declared bankrupt. Only death could stop his remorseless bad behaviour, and in the summer of 1957 it did. He died of gastroenteritis.

BRILLIANTINED BOB

As the bluffer can now confirm, bad behaviour and comedy are frequently easy bedfellows. But who would have thought that a well-known family entertainer would have such a saucy past? **Bob Monkhouse** was born in Beckenham, Kent in 1928. His grandfather had made a fortune in the custard powder industry but the young Monkhouse had no interest in going into the family business. By 17 he was performing comedy and big names, such as Max Miller, were buying his gags.

Monkhouse, however, may have been comedy's most unlikely Lothario, notching up various affairs during his first marriage. By the end of the 1940s, he was working on BBC radio with the voluptuous blonde starlet Diana Dors and was convinced there was some chemistry between them. In 1952, while his wife was away, he was invited to a party at Dors's house and accompanied a young dancer to a room with a mirror on the ceiling. But as he was disrobing, he heard giggling and realised that the mirror was two-way, and the other guests were on the other side watching. He grabbed his trousers and fled with the word 'homo' ringing in his ears, courtesy of the spurned showgirl. He later said of Dors's infamous parties: 'The awkward part about an orgy is that afterwards you're not too sure who to thank.'

It is frequently forgotten what a consummate stand-up

Monkhouse was, and bluffers should take the view that while he was undeniably corny, he was certainly in on his own joke. It would be invidious to choose any of his countless one-liners as wholly representative of his prodigious output, but that shouldn't stop you quoting one of his most famous: 'They laughed when I said I was going to be a comedian. Well, they're not laughing now.' He died in December 2003, aged 75. Like his hero Bob Hope, he joked until the end. 'You'll be glad to hear I can still enjoy sex at 74. I live at number 76. It's no distance.'

He even had a posthumous punchline. In 2007, thanks to computer trickery, he fronted an advert promoting prostate cancer awareness that ended on a typically corny gag: 'What killed me kills one man per hour in Britain. That's even more than my wife's cooking.'

CLUB CLASS

'Ah yes, I remember the good old days in the Chuckle Basket in Notting Hill where you could see five great acts, get drunk, pass out, and still have change from a tenner...' Battle-scarred comedy veterans will always talk about the great old gigs they went to. For rock fans it's the Sex Pistols at the 100 Club; for comedy fans, the holy grail was the original Comedy Store in Soho (*see* page 15).

Bluffers of the right vintage can convince anyone polite enough to listen that they were there by recalling those late nights when you went up to the venue in the matchbox-sized lift – just you, your friends and two confused Japanese businessmen thinking they were heading to one of Soho's steamier fleshpots.

Since those heady days of 1979, many more clubs have taken on legendary status. The first of these was **Jongleurs,** which went on to become a national chain but started out as a single club in a side street just off Lavender Hill above The Cornet pub, up the road from Clapham Junction. The room had originally been a banqueting hall called Stanley's

Restaurant before becoming Stanley's Masonic Hall. More recently it had been a roller disco.

The person who first opened it as a comedy club was Maria Kempinska. The daughter of Polish refugees, she had seen stand-up at the Edinburgh Fringe in 1982 and thought London needed more of the same. She pawned her bicycle and opened in February 1983. It was an instant success. The location and timing were perfect. This part of South London was the spiritual home of the nascent yuppie; they wanted to go out, have a laugh and throw money at the bar. Julian Clary, Rory Bremner, Jeremy Hardy, Harry Enfield and Jo Brand were among some of the early performers here. Some bluffers might claim to remember seeing Paul Merton and Eddie Izzard in a bizarre double act called The Entire Population of China where they engaged in combat dressed as cavaliers.

Jongleurs – the word usually means minstrel and not juggler as some think (never make that elementary mistake) – became a huge success. So much so, in fact, that if you stop someone in the street and ask them what jongleurs means today, they would probably say a riotous night out. You might venture that over the years, it has held over 60,000 comedy shows, and entertained (mostly) more than 11 million visitors.

ACROSS THE POND

The US comedy club boom slightly predated the British equivalent. On the other side of the Atlantic, however, the stand-up scene quickly became worryingly homogeneous and, shortly after it took off, the bubble burst. You should point out sagely that from the early days there were distinct artistic differences between the two principal countries of comedy. In the UK, the traditional ambition since the 1980s has been to put together a one-hour set to take to the Edinburgh Festival in the hope that the act might be discovered by TV producers. In the USA, things were much faster in every sense. A club act would focus on honing a breathless routine of less than 10 minutes designed to work for one of the hugely popular late-night talk shows – think of Robert De Niro as Rupert Pupkin in 1983's *The King of Comedy,* who ended up kidnapping a chat-show host to land a TV slot (note to any aspiring comedians: don't try this). These pocket-sized showcases could then be the springboards to getting signed up for a sitcom – preferably with your own name in the title. As cable TV took off, there were extended stand-up specials on HBO and Comedy Central, but for club comics these were a long way off.

Carolines is one of the most famous comedy clubs in New York, if not the world. Through its nondescript doors have walked some of the USA's most famous comedians, such as Jerry Seinfeld, Billy Crystal and Rosie O'Donnell. And, of course, you. Comedy fan Caroline Hirsch first opened the club in the Chelsea District in 1982. It was initially a cabaret venue, but as the comedy scene blossomed, stand-ups began to dominate, playing to small but appreciative audiences.

Hirsch was soon turning people away so she moved to bigger premises at New York's South Street Seaport district. Since 1992 the club has been on Broadway in Times Square in the very heart of Manhattan, just a couple of blocks from Radio City Music Hall, where various TV shows are recorded and where countless Carolines alumni have made their home. Point out to anybody interested (unlikely) that Carolines has no apostrophe, but then different rules apply over there.

Another legendary New York club is the **Comedy Cellar,** which naturally you will claim to know equally well, and which also opened in 1982. If you watch the sitcom *Louie*, point out that the gloomy, pizza-chewing comedian, played by Louis CK, is walking down the Comedy Cellar steps during the opening credits. The Cellar is in the heart of Greenwich Village, the once bohemian quarter of the city where so many comedy household names cut their teeth in the folk clubs in the 1960s. Chris Rock is among many stand-ups who have been known to road-test new material and flex their comedy muscles in this intimate space.

If you are a working comedian, though, you don't hang around at the back during a show; you hang around above the Cellar in the Olive Tree restaurant. In the corner, a TV relays the action onstage, giving the comics on the bill an idea of what the crowd is like and what material the acts going on before them are using. There is nothing worse than delivering a gag about a subject that is strikingly similar to one just done by the last act. Even if yours is better, you may be met by a groan from the crowd or, even worse, the cold grip of comedy's Grim Reaper as your snappy one-liner dies a horrible death through no fault of its own.

The real difference between American clubs and British clubs is not humour, however: it is alcohol consumption.

There are times in a British comedy club where it can feel as if a lot of people have gone out for a drink and the comedian has turned up and got in the way. In the USA, audiences tend to be more sober.

EXPLORING THE ID

One London club, however, has bucked the trend of boozy clubs in recent years and in the process has become the coolest comedy venue since the original Soho Comedy Store. The Invisible Dot, down a side street in King's Cross, is not just a club; it is a management company, a promoter, an agency and a producer. Effectively, it is more like a record label than a comedy club. The posters, flyers and adverts have a cohesive, thematic industrial design. In the comedy world, where most adverts look like they have been knocked out by a four-year-old with a box of crayons, this attention to detail sticks out a mile.

In 2009 'ID' promoted Tim Key and Jonny Sweet at the Edinburgh Festival. Key won the main Edinburgh Comedy Award and Sweet picked up the Best Newcomer Award. The agency's founder, Simon Pearce, is never less than creative. At the Edinburgh Festival in 2010, he installed four ex-BT phone boxes, bought in a job lot for £7,500, around the city. When you tried to make a call, there would be someone on the line – comedians Arthur Smith and Mark Watson or writer Will Self – reading out a story. ID also organised a strictly one-off comical mystery tour, entitled *By The Sea,* during which fans were bussed out of the city to the town hall across the road from Portobello Beach, where they were entertained by the likes of Kevin Eldon, Josie Long and Daniel Kitson.

ID didn't set out to be a fashionable comedy club but its acts needed somewhere to rehearse, so Pearce decided that the simplest solution was to push the desks in their Camden Town office to the side of the room and invite

♛

> At a lot of comedy clubs the performer stands against a brick wall – rather like facing a firing squad.

people to watch the acts perform in there. After a couple of years, the offices moved to King's Cross and this time the ground-floor room was given over to live shows. Walk through the large, brown, wooden barn doors and there is a bar right in front of you, and the gents and ladies are on either side of the stage at the front. Go to either during a performance and you may become part of the performance. But the performer is still the most vulnerable person in the room; comedy veteran Andy de la Tour once noted that at a lot of comedy clubs, the performer stands against a brick wall – rather like facing a firing squad.

The Invisible Dot venue only holds 75 people, but it attracts knowledgeable, committed and well-behaved comedy fans who like their laughs to be garnished with a generous sprinkling of absurdism. In other words, it is the bluffer's natural milieu. In

incorporate the call into their act. This generally results
n extensive humiliation of the mobile offender. Most
omedians are naturally adept at this form of casual cruelty.
Before the advent of the mobile phone, however, the
ivity most frowned upon in comedy clubs was the
ckle' – defined by the *Oxford English Dictionary* as 'to
rrupt with derisive or aggressive comments or abuse'.

e modern use of the term is said to have originated in
ee in the nineteenth century. This is useful information
e to hand in any conversation about stand-up comedy.
ng' originally meant to tease or comb out flax and
bres, and in the jute factories where this went on,
had to shout to be heard over the noise of the
y, so their shouting became known as 'heckling' as
hought that the workers who did the heckling then
ut angrily at visiting politicians on the campaign
might venture knowledgeably that these
ncluded a certain Winston Churchill, who sat
iberal MP from 1908 to 1922.) Over the years,
me known as 'heckling', too, and the pastime
ndoors to the music hall and variety theatres.
ndee's great gifts to the world. The others are
le and one of the finest comedy talents of the
espect Party politician 'Gorgeous' George
ot forgetting the pre-eminent British poet
ra, William McGonagall, once described
hat he backed unwittingly into genius').

any slip-up about stand-up or its provenance, you can simply
say: 'Everything and nothing changes – look at ID.' This, of
course, means absolutely nothing, but it'll give you breathing
space while you think of something better.

The aforementioned award-winner, self-proclaimed 'poet,
performer and savant' **Tim Key** – better known as Alan
Partridge's number two, Sidekick Simon (he was the one
strapped to a swivel chair with gaffer tape in the *Alpha
Papa* film) – performs regularly, delivering gnomic poetry,
sometimes with Russian pop music in the background.

You'll need to know that ID doesn't just stage stand-up
events, but also poetry and spoken-word nights. And if you
don't want to part with too much money, you should go to
its Edinburgh Fringe previews season every July. Not only
can you see stars of the future, but free burgers and pork
rolls are served in the interval. What's not to like?

ENTERING THE ARENA

London is spoilt for comedy clubs. There are clubs on boats,
clubs in disused factories, clubs in churches and, of course,
clubs in pubs. At the other end of the spectrum, there are the
arenas. Everyone should attend a comedy gig at the O2 Arena
on the Greenwich Peninsula once (but maybe only once). The
venue that was once the failed Millennium Dome and New
Labour's laughing stock has now become – rather fittingly –
the biggest comedy venue in the UK. Try not to be distracted
by the lure of hot dogs and cold lager; the important thing is
not to dismiss it out of hand. Instead, you might generously
say: 'Venues don't make or break stand-ups; bad acoustics

and crap material do.' Comedy aficionados will look at you with newfound respect.

Other arenas, now popping up all over the UK, are the kind of venues that are so large that if you're sitting at the back, you'll probably have to watch the acts on the large screens at the side of the stage. So you might just as well wait until the shows are released on DVD and watch in the comfort of your own home. And if you really want to replicate the arena experience, ask a friend to present you with a large bill for your hot dog and beer at the end of the evening while spilling half the drink and squirting some ketchup on your trousers.

NO HECKLING, PLEAS

There are rules to visiting a com
not be as arcane and codified a
or croquet, but rest assured th
get egg on your face and find that
are equally as important. In essen
that there are just two comedy c
very simple: enjoy the show an
mainly means don't talk and d
show. You may think you are
smartphone in your lap as
the fact that the people se
you, the light from the s
face and distracting th
Long has dubbed 'm

Mobile phones
Richard Herring
mobile miscrea
also pulverise
sometimes a
there's a risk

SPEAK ONLY WHEN SPOKEN TO

While hecklers have a rather irritating habit of believing that they are enhancing the act and helping them to have a good gig, you should point out that stand-up comedians almost universally hate them. Ben Elton developed his non-stop Gatling-gun delivery so that there was no pause to give a potential miscreant the space to interject. Maybe once in a while a witty interruption from the audience will bring a show to life, but more often than not they will flatten the momentum, ruin the atmosphere and make the performer and the rest of the auditorium feel a little uncomfortable.

Some clubs, such as Edinburgh's The Stand Comedy Club, have a zero-tolerance policy towards hecklers. One word out of line and you may find yourself out on the street regretting that moment when you failed to resist the temptation to articulate your thoughts out loud. Tommy Sheppard, director of The Stand, has put it fairly bluntly: 'At the risk of sounding like a Victorian dad, the golden rule is speak when spoken to.'

GLADIATORIAL COMBAT

It is rare for the audience to get the better of the performer. One really notable exception may be an urban myth, but one hopes it is true. Eric Douglas, the son of Kirk 'Spartacus' Douglas, was a stand-up comedian for a while and when doing a gig one night, the audience was giving him a hard time, so he said: 'You can't do this to me, I'm Kirk Douglas's son!' To which, one by one, the audience gradually piped up, in an echo of his father's famous film, 'No, I'm Kirk

Douglas's son… No, I'm Kirk Douglas's son… No, I'm Kirk Douglas's son…'

The Spartacus reference was more appropriate than they realised; there is something gladiatorial about a heckler taking on a comedian. It would rarely happen in any other art form. Was Olivier ever heckled when doing his Henry V? Would you heckle a movie? Would a ballerina ever be told to get off the stage for being rubbish? Yet in comedy, an art form with the flimsiest of fourth walls, the heckler will insist on taking on the performer and risk, if not annihilation, then certainly humiliation.

TUNNEL EFFECT

The comedy venue that was most famous for the ferocity of its hecklers was the Tunnel Club in London's Greenwich. The Tunnel ran for a few glorious, anarchic years in the mid-1980s. Legend has it that one night Jim Tavaré opened his act with the line: 'Good evening, I'm a schizophrenic.' Someone immediately shouted 'Fuck off then, both of you.' But first-rate banter like this that increases rather than decreases the fun is the exception. Comedy producer Toby Jones once said that asking a comedian if they like hecklers is akin to asking someone if they like motorists: 'Some are good, but mostly they get in the way of an enjoyable trip.'

The Tunnel Club was run by the late legendary maverick Malcolm Hardee who, while he did not actively promote heckling, hardly had the same hatred of it as the director of The Stand. Instead, he had his own distinctive way of dealing with disruptive elements in his club. He once saw an audience member drunkenly snoring so went over to him, unzipped his fly and urinated into the man's pint.

MASTERFUL REJOINDERS

Over the years, comedians have honed their skills at dealing with hecklers. Simply asking hecklers politely to desist may only encourage them. Somehow, noisy elements have to be reminded that stand-up comedy is generally a monologue, not a duologue. Unless, of course, the performer actively invites audience participation – as many of them do.

'I remember when I had my first pint'
is a tried and trusted response
when one hears an offensive grunt from
the dark recesses of the stalls.

A smart put-down is the response preferred by most seasoned professionals. Some lines work better than others and can be adjusted to suit different occasions. 'I remember when I had my first pint' is a tried-and-trusted response when one hears an offensive grunt from the dark recesses of the stalls.

The psychology of hecklers is not always easily understood. Some are show-offs trying to impress their chums, some are attention-seekers, some are drunk, some may be suffering from self-esteem issues. Sometimes all four. Rest assured that they rarely improve a performance. Sometimes a persistent heckler can make the rest of the audience too tense to enjoy the performance. Can the stand-up respond? Can they hold their own? A withering put-down might make the comedian look better, of course, but on balance most comedians would prefer there to be no hecklers and simply to be allowed to deliver the material they've prepared and perfected unimpeded by over-refreshed amateurs.

The worst hecklers are those just out to cause trouble. They don't really care about the quality of the act; they just think they have something valuable to say. Some apologists for hecklers say that at least it means that they are paying attention – though maybe not always quite enough attention. There is a story of a group of comedians standing at the back of a club one night, when someone who has been heckling all evening comes up to one of them and says: 'You were shit.' To which the comedian pointed out: 'Er, I've not actually been on yet.'

Female comedians have had particular problems with hecklers in recent years. There was a time when a woman would only have to walk onstage and some oaf in the audience would shout 'Get 'em off' or 'Show us your tits.' This has, thankfully, become less of an issue in recent years – partly because audiences are more enlightened and partly because women rapidly mastered the art of the witty response. When someone called Jo Brand fat she replied: 'I deliberately keep my weight up so that a tosser like you won't fancy me.' The late comedian Linda Smith also had a nifty response to a request to reveal her breasts: 'Why? Is it time for your feed?'

The attentive bluffer may have observed by now that one of the smartest attitudes to adopt in the face of bovine stupidity is one of intellectual superiority. The comedian will immediately get the rest of the audience on their side and make the heckler feel stupid. Jack Dee has been known to use a very succinct line: 'Well, it's a night out for him… and a night off for his family.'

It is the smart rejoinder that usually wins the day. The stand-up should resist, if at all possible, the temptation to succumb to the gutter level of the less eloquent punter. A sophisticated return volley will invariably win the point.

However, Rufus Hound, who wrote a book about the subject in 2011, *Stand Up Put Downs,* doesn't think there is much point in subtlety. He has called his approach 'blunt-force trauma'. Hit them harder than they have hit you. One of his favourite all-purpose put-downs when there is a noisy element in the room is to call over to the bar staff and ask: 'Can we get some crayons and a menu for this guy to colour in please?'

Comedians often claim not to care about winning awards, but one suspects that they feel differently once they do.

FEASTS OF COMEDY

I f you have unlimited funds, no commitments and plenty of time on your hands, you could spend the entire year, if not an entire lifetime, travelling the world enjoying different comedy festivals. In recent years the comedian's calendar has become positively peppered with festivals. Each has distinctive personalities, and if you claim to know anything about stand-up you'll need to know what's happening where and when, and what to say about it.

The comedy festival season starts and ends and then starts all over again with the Edinburgh Festival Fringe, which takes place over three weeks in August. Depending on the vicissitudes of the Gregorian calendar and bank holiday dates, it can start as early as the end of July or conclude at the very start of September – though not in the same year. Only a regular would know that, so put it in your bluffing bank.

The Fringe started in 1947 as an antidote to the mainstream Edinburgh International Festival, established in the same year, which set out to showcase music, dance, visual arts, theatre… and a load of other cultural highlights that didn't include comedy. It was a slow start; the original Fringe festival had only one page of events listed. The 2014 Fringe programme would barely fit through a letterbox, which is why it is now increasingly online and available as an app. Other festivals are held simultaneously in Edinburgh over the summer celebrating film, TV, books and science (actually, that's in April), and they all come under the umbrella term Edinburgh Festival, of which the Fringe is an independently run part. You'll be safe in contending that it is now the biggest comedy festival in the world, by some distance.

Even as recently as 1981, when the Perrier Award for Comedy started, there were only around 40 comedy shows on the Fringe, and most of those were of the old-school cabaret and revue style – not really very Fringe at all, compared to the hotbed of anarchic alternative stand-up bubbling up in London in the early 1980s. The first Perrier winners, the Cambridge Footlights, including Emma Thompson, Stephen Fry and Hugh Laurie, did not have much competition, but they still seem to have done pretty well for themselves.

IT'S NOT AS GOOD AS IT WAS

By the mid-1980s more comedians were heading to Edinburgh in search of fame, fortune and French mineral water. In 1987 Arnold (catchphrase: 'Why not...?') Brown was the first real alternative comedy stand-up to win the Perrier Award, sharing it with cabaret act Barb Jungr and Michael Parker who provided musical accompaniment to the show *Brown Blues*. But soon stand-ups filled the whole hour themselves. By the early 1990s the trickle had become a flood, with Sean Hughes (1990), Frank Skinner (1991), Steve

Coogan (1992) and Lee Evans (1993) among the winners. Hughes was the youngest-ever winner at the time – just 24 when he won it for his show in which he spent an hour in his imaginary flat dreaming that Morrissey might call him.

Since the early 1990s, the Edinburgh Comedy Awards has had a succession of different sponsors, which you'll need to know about – because the subject is guaranteed to come up at some stage. The Perrier briefly became the if.comedy awards; then in 2009 it had no sponsor at all (but its original director/producer, Nica Burns, footed the bill. Aspiring comedians everywhere should drink a toast to her for doing so). Since then, Australian lager brand Foster's

♔

Every year the old hands will say that Edinburgh is not as good as it once was.

has been on board. In other respects, some things have thankfully remained constant. Comedians have always moaned about how much money they lose attending the Fringe, but they keep coming back. They often claim not to care about winning awards, but one suspects that they feel differently once they do.

Another racing certainty – apart from the fact that there will be a biblical downpour at some point during the festival – is that every year the old hands will say that Edinburgh is not as good as it once was, that it is too cynical and career-orientated, that the art has gone out of it and that it is not as funny as it once was. Any bluffer claiming to be an Edinburgh veteran must repeat this mantra within the first five minutes of any conversation about the Fringe. It's an article of faith.

DON'T MENTION THE MOOSE

Yet if anyone does think that the Edinburgh Fringe has become over-commercialised, they should cast an eye at the Just For Laughs Festival which takes place in Montreal in July. There used to be something called the US Comedy Arts Festival in Aspen, Colorado, but since 2005 it has been renamed The Comedy Festival and transplanted to Las Vegas. A US counterpart to the Montreal Just for Laughs had established a foothold in Chicago, but in 2013 after five years running, organizers pulled the plug. Montreal remains the big one and traditionally the place where American TV executives head to spot talent. And because of that, it has become vital for every stand-up with a semblance of ambition to attend.

The business-oriented culture often surprises some of the more innocent-abroad comics, though. Campaigning comedian Mark Thomas made his debut in Montreal in 1992. He recalls having a relaxing soak in a Jacuzzi when an agent passed him his business card – laminated so that it wouldn't be damaged by the water. These days, the agent would be busy sending his contact details on a water-resistant smartphone.

Some British acts have had difficulties in Montreal where their distinctive humour has not always translated as intended. In 1993, at the height of their fame in the UK, Vic Reeves and Bob Mortimer went to Montreal and performed their song 'Lucky Carpet' (about Vic's favourite 30ft lucky charm) to a sea of bemused faces and dropped jaws. (To be honest, there was much the same reaction back home.) In 1991 the outrageous Jerry Sadowitz came on and said: 'Good evening, moose fuckers'. Shortly afterwards he was punched by an irate audience member.

If Montreal is about the business and Edinburgh is about the art, the Melbourne International Comedy Festival comes somewhere in between, maybe with one eye on Edinburgh. The festival runs for four weeks across March and April. Like Edinburgh, there are prizes for the best shows; in Melbourne they are known as the Barrys and winners have included Ross Noble (2002), Daniel Kitson (2007), Russell Kane (2011) and Dr Brown (2012). (The largely silent American comedian Phil Burgers then took his 'Dr Brown' character to the Edinburgh Fringe and won the Foster's Award there, too.)

A big difference between Melbourne and Edinburgh, however, is that Edinburgh is accessible to anyone who can find a place to perform; you have to be invited to Melbourne. The advantage of this is that once invited, you certainly get looked after and pampered in a way that never happens in Scotland. You're put up in nice accommodation, you're ferried to and from your gigs; you could probably even get them to do your laundry if you ask nicely. And the weather's pretty good, too.

There is a strong element of competitiveness in Melbourne and Edinburgh, which you might point out is not quite so evident at the Kilkenny Cat Laughs Comedy Festival. This Irish cultural highlight was founded in 1994 and takes place in various pubs and theatres in the small city over the first weekend in June. There is no prize, no publicity campaign, and what few agents are there keep a low profile.

More recently, there's the new joker on the block: the Altitude Festival in Mayrhofen, Austria, which combines stand-up comedy with fall-down Alpine skiing*. Altitude originally started in Meribel in France. A group of comedians including Marcus Brigstocke and Andrew Maxwell used to do gigs out there in return for free skiing and snowboarding. Gradually, more comedians got wind of the perk and it was decided that the only way to accommodate them all was to start a festival. After a few years in Meribel, it moved to Mayrhofen. Without wishing to endanger the Entente Cordiale, the Austrians seem to have a better grip on the British sense of humour than the French. In Mayrhofen the likes of John Bishop, Eddie Izzard and Tim Minchin have played to sell-out audiences. Jenny Eclair did one of the early Altitudes but had not done much skiing before, so wore shocking pink nail polish on the basis that if she got buried in the snow she could stick her hand out and attract the attention of a friendly mountain rescue dog. Nobody had told her that if you do get caught, the snow compacts around you like cement and you can't move a muscle. Your best chance of being located by a sniffer dog is having a pocketful of Cheesy Wotsits.

*See *The Bluffer's Guide to Skiing* to learn how to fall over and pretend you did it on purpose.

The aforementioned is by no means a comprehensive list of festivals around the world. There are many others in the UK alone. Brighton hosts a jolly autumnal shindig where the Edinburgh hits can bring their sets to the Sussex coast. Every May, Machynlleth in Wales now also has a boutique-style rival to Kilkenny. Any town with a comedy club will usually rustle up enough gigs to justify a festival. In 2013 there were also festivals in Chippenham, Stourbridge, Birmingham, Glasgow, Belfast, Liverpool, Hull, Sunderland, Newport, Stratford-upon-Avon, Cardiff, Bristol, Bath, Belfast, Nottingham and Manchester. The Leicester Comedy Festival – which claims to be the oldest in England – had a particularly high profile in 2013, as it coincided with the discovery of King Richard III's skeleton in a council car park near one of the venues. The organisers quickly came up with their own 'Funny Bones' adverts.

In London in one month in 2013, there were festivals in Balham and Ealing and two different ones in Camden Town. Countries with English-speaking populations are always keen to host comedy events; there have been festivals in places as far apart as Singapore, New Zealand and South Africa. Carolines Comedy Club has organised a New York Comedy Festival every year since 2004. In fact, even countries where English is not the first language are getting in on the act. In January, Norway's capital Oslo plays host to the Crap Comedy Festival. The emphasis here is on absurdist and political comedians. In 2013 the line-up included Josie Long, Robin Ince and Daniel Kitson. No awards, no prizes, no TV deals. Just a stand-up and a stage.

These days a token British or Irish comedian seems to be an essential ingredient when casting an American movie.

STAND-UP GOES
TO HOLLYWOOD

This wasn't in the script. Just when you think British stand-up comedians can't get any bigger, they go and lay siege to Hollywood. The smart bluffer should always make the point that, unlike rock stars, stand-up comedians make excellent actors. Sting v Jerry Seinfeld? David Bowie v Woody Allen? Mick Jagger v Billy Connolly? Case closed.

And it is easier for a comedian to play a serious role than for a serious actor to play a comedian. Tom Hanks tried to play one in the film *Punchline*. Hanks is actually a pretty good actor. He can convince you that he is an astronaut, a ship's captain, a 13-year-old boy – even a stetson-wearing toy cowboy called Woody. But he couldn't convince you that he was a stand-up comedian. Robert De Niro (before he descended into self-parody) did a much better job in *The King of Comedy*, but it was still hard to get past the knowledge that this was the same actor who played young Vito Corleone in *The Godfather Part II* with a similar moustache – albeit this time wearing a silly jacket and a bow tie.

In the USA, modern stand-up comedians have regularly

made the journey from stage to screen. The trend was begun by music-hall stars such as WC Fields and Buster Keaton, helped by British expats like Charlie Chaplin and Stan Laurel. Countless American stand-ups have become Hollywood A-listers after cutting their teeth in clubs rather than drama schools.

Robin Williams made the transition – so did Steve Martin, Richard Pryor and Jim Carrey, among others. Various alumni of the American TV sketch comedy show *Saturday Night Live* then reached the big screen, including Bill Murray, Mike Myers, John Belushi, Dan Aykroyd and Will Ferrell. A number of hit films even grew out of *SNL* sketches including *The Blues Brothers* and *Wayne's World*. Eddie Murphy and Chris Rock are notable examples of comics who became major movie stars. Chris Tucker went from being a stand-up to one of Hollywood's highest-paid movie stars following his success in the *Rush Hour* franchise. He reportedly banked a $25 million cheque for *Rush Hour 3* in 2006.

These successes weren't that unusual. The performers had huge fan bases in the USA already, so the move into films was no major surprise. What has been more unexpected in recent years is the number of British stand-ups making the move to Hollywood .

HEAD BRAND

While Perrier Award winners Hugh Laurie and Stephen Fry have had their share of exposure in the USA – Laurie principally on TV's *House* but also as a talking cockroach in the animated *Monsters v Aliens,* Fry everywhere from *The Hobbit* to *Wilde* – Russell Brand is the most high-profile British comedian in recent years to have set his sights on Hollywood. His supporting role as rock star Aldous Snow

---

♛

Russell Brand's cinematic oeuvre often involves 'playing versions of myself – sometimes with a hat on'.

---

in *Forgetting Sarah Marshall* made such an impact that an entire movie, *Get Him to The Greek,* was built around the philandering adventurer's character (Snow, not Brand, but it is easy to get confused). Brand then played a similar character but with more of a drink problem in the remake of the Dudley Moore vehicle, *Arthur.* It was a genuinely terrible film. As Brand said himself during his *Messiah Complex* stage show, his cinematic oeuvre often involves 'playing versions of myself – sometimes with a hat on'.

AFTER *THE OFFICE*

Having made it as a stand-up relatively late in life, Ricky Gervais has made up for lost time with a succession of big-screen projects. You will appear better informed, however, if you state, correctly, that none of his films have been quite as cleverly observed as his TV sitcom *The Office.* You might also add that he can often be found playing versions of himself, too – sometimes with a beard on.

In *Ghost Town* (2008) Gervais played a dentist who has a near-death experience and afterwards can see ghosts and has to spend his time helping them sort out their problems. In the quietly subversive *The Invention Of Lying* (2009), he even brought his own atheistic beliefs to the big screen in a romcom about a parallel world where everybody is painfully honest in all situations. Gervais's character tells the first lie and eventually comes up with the idea of Man In The Sky – God – which he then reveals is a lie. This had an echo of his own upbringing. 'My mum only lied to me about one thing. She said there was a God. But that's because when you're a working-class mum, Jesus is like an unpaid babysitter,' he has said.

Gervais has arguably made more of a mark as the host of the Golden Globes from 2010 to 2012 – even if the joke about insulting Hollywood stars to their faces probably started to wear a bit thin. And you can show how much you know your subject by pointing out that Dennis Pennis (the much-underrated comedian and actor Paul Kaye) was doing it to toe-curlingly, painfully embarrassing effect 20 years ago.

Even Gervais's less extroverted writing partner Stephen Merchant has had a taste of Hollywood fame, appearing most prominently in the children's film *Tooth Fairy* – though at six feet seven inches, he's pretty prominent wherever he appears. Merchant has co-written one of the most famous sitcoms of all time, had a successful tour of his stand-up show *Hello Ladies* (which later landed him an HBO series of the same name), but it isn't comedy fans who stare at him in the street: 'I get recognised by families who get excited because their kids have made them watch me in *Tooth Fairy* eight times that day.'

A PARTRIDGE IN TINSELTOWN

Ricky Gervais also cropped up as the grouchy museum director in *Night at the Museum*, a film that also gave a role to another British comedian who has made repeated attempts to break into the Hollywood mainstream. Steve Coogan played a miniature Roman warrior who forged an alliance with Owen Wilson's equally vertically challenged cowboy. There was more of a hint of Coogan's crass Alan Partridge about this performance, but then there has been a hint of Partridge about a lot of Coogan's work. His Tony Wilson in *24 Hour Party People* felt at times like Partridge running a record label, and his Paul Raymond in *The Look of Love* felt at times like Partridge as a porn baron.

The 2002 film *24 Hour Party People,* about how Tony Wilson founded Manchester's Factory Records, helped Coogan pick up a cult following in the USA. Ben Stiller and Jack Black were fans and he went on to appear with them in the deeply flawed *Tropic Thunder*. The BBC series *The Trip* also helped Coogan's profile. An edited version of the six-part series, in which he played a version of himself reviewing jus-infused restaurants in the Lake District, was turned into a feature for a movie release on the other side of the Atlantic. Coogan may finally be breaking through. 21 years after playing Partridge in his Perrier Award-winning show, the

Pringle-jumpered pratfaller made it into the cinema in his own right in *Alan Partridge: Alpha Papa*. And his acclaimed 2013 film, *Philomena*, found him playing it straight as TV reporter Martin Sixsmith. One could barely see a hint of Partridge. Honest.

ALWAYS THE BRIDESMAID

These days, a token British or Irish comedian seems to be an essential ingredient when casting an American movie. Genial Irish actor and comedian Chris O'Dowd, of *The IT Crowd* fame, appeared in the 2011 romcom *Bridesmaids* (which was surprisingly good). Although he has never performed as a comedian onstage, he qualifies for inclusion because of his role as a stand-up in the 2005 film *Festival*. His *IT Crowd* co-star Richard Ayoade (Perrier Award winner in 2001 as part of Garth Marenghi's *Netherhead*) then co-starred with Ben Stiller in *The Watch* (2012).

Meanwhile, Matt Lucas appeared in *Bridesmaids* and had two bites of the cherry as Tweedledum and, in a piece of frankly inspired casting, also as Tweedledee in Tim Burton's version of *Alice in Wonderland*. Lucas's partner in *Little Britain,* David Walliams, has also dipped a toe across the Atlantic, appearing as a camp German alongside Steve Carell in *Dinner For Schmucks* (2010), as well as playing a minor role in the romantic fantasy *Stardust* (2007), which also featured Gervais.

ZOM-ROMCOM

One of the most successful comedians-turned-film-actors is Simon Pegg. In the 1990s Pegg was a character comic and, with Julia Davies, was Steve Coogan's touring support act, filling in the gaps while Coogan was changing costumes. He quickly graduated to cinema after hit TV sitcom *Spaced* by making the hugely successful zom-romcom *Shaun of the Dead* (2004). The success opened numerous doors.

He continued his own so-called Cornetto Trilogy with director Edgar Wright and former Mexican restaurant waiter Nick Frost by making *Hot Fuzz* (2007) and *The World's End* (2013), but Pegg has also become an in-demand actor with an appealing comic touch, sometimes supporting in blockbusters – Scotty in the *Star Trek* reboots – sometimes playing the lead in smaller films – *Paul* and *Run Fatboy Run*. There was a rare failure when he played the lead role opposite Kirsten Dunst in the undistinguished comedy *How to Lose Friends & Alienate People* (2008), but you can't win everything.

You'll be on safe ground remarking that Pegg has been the British comedian who has had the most film success in America. He has built up an enviable track record that nobody could have predicted when he was trying to keep an audience of Steve Coogan fans from getting restless. Because Pegg has been so successful elsewhere, it is easy to forget he was once a stand-up. But he earned his spurs onstage with the best of them, facing an audience and working hard for a laugh. So he qualifies.

BELIEVE IT, OR NOT

Others have tried to carve out a movie career with less success. The uniquely talented Eddie Izzard has been a successful stand-up comedian all over the world, but you might observe that he'd probably prefer to draw a discreet veil over his film career. Whether it's just downright bad luck or some kind of curse is hard to say, but Izzard seems to have had more encounters with lifeless turkeys than Bernard Matthews. He had small parts in *Ocean's Twelve* and *Ocean's Thirteen* but he has only really had star billing in one film. You can draw your own conclusions from this, but the film Izzard has been the most convincing in is *Believe* (2009), which was a documentary about his life. It was clearly a role he was born to play.

There's no point in pretending that you know everything about stand-up comedy – nobody does (least of all those of us who write about it for a living). But if you've got this far and you've absorbed at least a modicum of the information and advice contained within these pages, then you will almost certainly know more than 99% of the rest of the human race about what stand-up is, how it started, who does it best, where they do it, why people enjoy it and how you can pretend to know more about it than you do. What you now do with this information is up to you, but here's a suggestion: be confident about your newfound knowledge, see how far it takes you but, above all, have fun using it. You are now a fully fledged expert in one of mankind's oldest and most addictive pleasures, otherwise known as the spontaneous eruption of unarticulated sounds often described as laughter.

Oh, and never be tempted to heckle someone mid-performance. Stand-ups can be as merciless as professional assassins and twice as sadistic. They can destroy you with one blow of their tongue but – like a cat with a mouse – not before they've had a bit of fun with you first.

**Think you're ready to shine with
your knowledge of stand-up comedy?
Test it first with our quiz at bluffers.com.**

GLOSSARY

Bomb *See* 'Die'.

Callbacks Otherwise known as 'back references', this is when a comedian mentions a subject early in their routine, then towards the end brings things full circle and amazes the audience by mentioning it again just when they least expect it.

Catchphrase Any collection of words that can raise a laugh simply by being repeated at every performance. Still popular on TV in sitcoms and sketch shows, and once a staple of live stand-up comedy performance, catchphrases seem to have fallen out of favour, but there are a few that are still going strong, such as The Pub Landlord's 'Glass of white wine for the lady' or, in expanded form, 'Pint for the gent, white wine or fruit-based drink for the lady.'

Corporates Private gigs done for huge amounts of money rather than artistic satisfaction. Anything from hosting an industry awards evening to a Russian oligarch's New Year's Eve party. The latter usually pays better, but there could be catastrophic misunderstandings of a cultural nature.

Cotton mouth Also known as dry-mouth syndrome – the horrible moment when nerves get the better of you and your entire body seems to dehydrate in a split second. There is rarely any coming back from this. The best thing is to leave the stage as soon as you are able to muster another laugh. Assuming you can still speak, that is.

Deconstruction A comedy routine in which part of the joke is that the comedian is explaining what the joke is or how it should work. Stewart Lee is the master of this, but it has now become so common that it is on the cusp of becoming a hack subject itself. (*See* below.)

Decoy assumption Setting up a certain expectation of a gag, i.e., that the story is about being at home having sex with your partner before the 'pull back and reveal' technique (*see* below) puts what you have just said in a different, hopefully funnier, context, i.e., you were on the upper deck of an open-top tourist bus.

Die Rather self-explanatory – to be onstage and fail to make people laugh. *See* also 'Bomb'.

Doubling up Not doubling up with laughter. 'Doubling up' is the practice of doing more than one gig in a night to increase one's earnings. In London it is possible to open the early show at the Comedy Store, rush across London to do another gig, and return for the Comedy Store's late show. This is technically tripling up. Hal Cruttenden is the Usain Bolt of gigging; he has been known to manage five gigs in a night.

Flop sweat The horrible thing about the human body is that if things are going badly onstage you may dry up (*see* 'Cotton mouth') – but your body may choose to do the exact opposite and go into a flop sweat, covering you in an instant layer of perspiration. Not a pretty sight and no amount of tissues will dry you up entirely. Again, the best advice is to get a laugh and leave.

Gag hag A rather unsavoury term for a woman who follows comedians around. Not quite the same as a groupie; a gag hag might be more of a hanger-on than a sleeping partner.

Hack Jokes that cover well-trodden terrain; examples are airport security and self-service checkouts. Can also be used to describe a comedian whose material is unoriginal, i.e., 'He's such a hack…'

Kill The opposite of 'Die' – to have great success. *See* also 'Storm', 'Slam'.

Mobile phone blue face The interesting phenomenon of someone's face being illuminated by the mobile phone in their lap.

Nail *See* 'Slam'.

Open mic A gig that allows amateurs to have a go at stand-up at their peril. Never a good idea without careful preparation.

Open spot A step up from open mic, this is a chance for a comedian who has a little more experience to try out a more professional environment. Probably unpaid, though if they do well they might get a paid booking from the same club.

Pull back and reveal The moment at the end of a joke when an unexpected turn makes it funny. Often these can be a little hack – i.e., 'It wouldn't have been so bad if it hadn't been my mum.' Also known as 'reversal'. *See* also 'Decoy assumption'.

Reversal *See* 'Pull back and reveal'.

Rule of three The rhythm of comedy makes a list of three things much funnier than a list of just two or a list of four… hence 'an Englishman, an Irishman and a Scotsman'. Never 'an Englishman and a Scotsman', or 'an Englishman, an Irishman, a Welshman and a Scotsman'.

Schtick Yiddish word that has come to mean 'style', as in: 'He always does that. That's his schtick.'

Segue The magical link that helps one move seamlessly between two bits of a set.

Slam When a comedian deals with a heckler with such a devastatingly smart put-down that there can be no response from the fan except to shrivel in their seat like a salted snail. *See* also 'Nail' and 'Kill'.

Storm *See* 'Kill'.

Tag line Additional punchline.

Zinger A brilliant joke guaranteed to make everyone laugh so much that they find it difficult to breathe.

BLUFFING NOTES

Bluffing Notes

Bluffing Notes

Bluffing Notes

Bluffing Notes

Bluffing Notes

Bluffing Notes

Bluffing Notes

ABOUT THE AUTHOR

BRUCE DESSAU has been a comedy fan for as long as he can remember and a critic for almost as long. He has seen more stand-up gigs than he has had hot dinners, though that may be because he has missed a lot of hot dinners due to being at stand-up gigs. He has chaired the Edinburgh Comedy Awards panel twice and has regularly served on the judging committee, trawling the Scottish capital every summer in search of new talent. He has talked about comedians on TV and radio and written about them for *The Guardian* and *The Times*. He is currently the comedy critic for the *London Evening Standard*. He is the editor of comedy website Beyond The Joke and the author of numerous books including biographies of Reeves and Mortimer and Rowan Atkinson. When not reviewing gigs, he can usually be found lurking at the back of stand-up clubs for his own amusement. His favourite comedian is publicity-shy genius Daniel Kitson.